T0112952

Overcoming Oppositional Defiant Disorder

OVERCOMING
Oppositional Defiant Disorder

A ***Two-Part*** Treatment Plan
to Help Parents and Kids
Work ***Together***

Gina Atencio-MacLean, PsyD

ALTHEA
PRESS

Copyright © 2019 by Althea Press, Emeryville, California

No part of this publication may be reproduced, stored in a retrieval system, or trans-mitted in any form or by any means, electronic, mechanical, photocopying, recording, scanning, or otherwise, except as permitted under Sections 107 or 108 of the 1976 United States Copyright Act, without the prior written permission of the Publisher. Requests to the Publisher for permission should be addressed to the Permissions Department, Althea Press, 6005 Shellmound Street, Suite 175, Emeryville, CA 94608.

Limit of Liability/Disclaimer of Warranty: The Publisher and the author make no representations or warranties with respect to the accuracy or completeness of the contents of this work and specifically disclaim all warranties, including without limitation warranties of fitness for a particular purpose. No warranty may be created or extended by sales or promotional materials. The advice and strategies contained herein may not be suitable for every situation. This work is sold with the understand-ing that the Publisher is not engaged in rendering medical, legal, or other professional advice or services. If professional assistance is required, the services of a competent professional person should be sought. Neither the Publisher nor the author shall be liable for damages arising herefrom. The fact that an individual, organization, or website is referred to in this work as a citation and/or potential source of further information does not mean that the author or the Publisher endorses the informa-tion the individual, organization, or website may provide or recommendations they/it may make. Further, readers should be aware that Internet websites listed in this work may have changed or disappeared between when this work was written and when it is read.

For general information on our other products and services or to obtain technical support, please contact our Customer Care Department within the U.S. at (866) 744-2665, or outside the U.S. at (510) 253-0500.

Althea Press publishes its books in a variety of electronic and print formats. Some content that appears in print may not be available in electronic books, and vice versa.

TRADEMARKS: Althea Press and the Althea Press logo are trademarks or registered trademarks of Callisto Media Inc. and/or its affiliates, in the United States and other countries, and may not be used without written permission. All other trademarks are the property of their respective owners. Althea Press is not associated with any product or vendor mentioned in this book.

Interior and Cover Designer: Will Mack
Editor: Camille Hayes
Production Editor: Andrew Yackira

ISBN: Print 978-1-64152-237-3 | eBook 978-1-64152-238-0

Contents

To my dad, Johnny Atencio,
who was labeled "incorrigible,"
and my mom, Betty,
who loved him anyway.

To Sandy and Liam,
my two great loves.

Introduction

LET ME BEGIN BY CONGRATULATING YOU ON YOUR COURAGE in trying a new approach to helping your child manage their oppositional behavior. If your child has been formally diagnosed with oppositional defiant disorder (ODD), then I can safely assume that they—and your whole family—have been struggling for a while. As a clinical psychologist who specializes in treating children and adolescents with behavioral problems, I know parenting a child with ODD is hard! It can be very difficult to keep your cool in the face of your child's explosive behavior. By the time most parents come into my office for help, their child's oppositional behaviors have been present for some time and are continuing to intensify, with no end in sight. If this sounds familiar, you've come to the right place.

This book is a bit different from other parenting books on ODD. Part one is dedicated entirely to tools and strategies for managing the emotional demands of parenting a "prickly" child. In other words, part one teaches you how to take care of *you*. This is important because it takes a lot of consistency, patience, and effort to help your child acquire the skills they lack. You cannot do this if you don't properly care for your own emotional and physical well-being.

Part two of this book focuses on concrete ways to help your child learn the skills to function more successfully in life. It's a systematic program that targets unhelpful behaviors for reduction and increases desired behaviors. The assumption in this model is that your child is not a bad kid—they just have skills deficits in some very important areas. I truly believe that most children with ODD can learn to manage their symptoms more effectively.

This book is not a quick fix. As you probably already know, there is no such thing when it comes to ODD. I encourage you to work your way through this book at a comfortable pace, taking the time to really absorb new information and try the suggested strategies. Do all the exercises—try not to skip over any of them. It doesn't matter how fast you get to the end. What's important is how well you integrate the tools and practices into your daily life. Though I can't give you an exact time frame for working through this book, I'd estimate that it should take several months if you're following the whole program as written. That's not to say it will take that long to start seeing results, but it will take at least that long to complete all of the exercises and action plans.

A few brief notes: All references to clients in this book are based on composites of previous cases, and all potentially identifying information has been changed. I use terms like *ODD child* and *child with ODD* interchangeably for ease of reading, not to imply that a child is defined by their ODD diagnosis. I use the term *parents* to refer to the adult caregivers in a child's life for the same reason, not to imply any disrespect for the roles of stepparents, foster parents, grandparents, and so on.

PART ONE

Taking Care of You

CHAPTER ONE

The Two-Part Program

Parenting a Child with ODD

Let's face it: Parenting is hard under the best conditions. Parenting a child who struggles with oppositional behavior is even more challenging. I know because I work with families whose kids have been diagnosed with oppositional defiant disorder (ODD). By the time most families come into my office, they've been trying to manage their child's behavior for years, with little to no improvement. They're exhausted, distressed, and desperate to help their child.

And they're facing pretty tough conditions at home. Parents report being verbally and physically assaulted by their kids, worrying about the safety and well-being of their other children, and having real concerns about their child being expelled from school. Additionally, many parents have overwhelming feelings of shame and fear being judged or blamed for their kid's behavior.

The stress that parents face on a daily basis takes a toll on them emotionally, physically, and cognitively. According to the National Institute of Mental Health, prolonged stress can lead to increased rates of physical illness, serious health problems, and mental health concerns like depression and anxiety. That's why this book—in addition to teaching you strategies to help your child—aims to give you tools to manage your own stress in healthy and practical ways.

One of the main complaints I hear from parents of kids with ODD is that they feel they're always "on edge," always waiting for the other shoe to drop, for the next outburst to shatter their calm. Psychologists call this on-edge feeling *hypervigilance*. Our brains use hypervigilance to help us stay safe by constantly scanning our environment for threats. This is very useful if we're out in the forest where there are lots of hungry bears, but not so helpful when we're helping our child with homework at the kitchen table. Unfortunately, a brain under stress often cannot tell the difference.

Another word for a threat is *trigger*. A trigger is the thing that, when it crops up—either in your environment or as an internal thought or feeling—engages your stress response and all the unpleasant things that go with it: racing heart, racing thoughts, anxiety, panic, even rage. Triggers for parents of children with ODD are usually related to their kids' acting-out behaviors, such as tantrums, aggression, and defiance. Once you're triggered, it's hard to respond calmly to your child, because your brain is telling you they're a threat to your physical and psychological well-being.

Imagine that your child comes home from school and starts complaining about homework. You begin to feel tense and anxious, anticipating the daily battle over long division. Your mind races with images of yesterday's homework time, and you have thoughts like *I know he's going to throw a tantrum* and *I hope she doesn't hit anyone this time*. Your child, whose brain is also wired to detect threats, gets triggered in return, and the usual pattern of chaos ensues. Neither you nor your child wants this outcome; it's simply become a pattern of reacting in habitual ways to the signals your brains have both detected. The goal for you is to learn skills to counteract these triggers, so you can meet your child's ODD symptoms with patience, empathy, and consistency.

The Oxygen Mask Dilemma

Have you ever noticed how flight attendants instruct parents to put on their own oxygen masks before their child's in case of an emergency? That's because if a parent is incapacitated—whether by anxiety, stress, or oxygen deprivation—they cannot meet their child's needs.

What's true for the airline passenger is true for the parent struggling with their child's ODD. As you've probably noticed, if your stress, anxiety, shame, or anger is getting triggered regularly, you likely aren't helping your child as much as you want. Since you're choosing to read this book, I can make some assumptions about you: (1) You love your child very much, (2) you would do anything to help them, and (3) you're under significant stress and so are not functioning at your best. The other thing I know is that you want to do better. You want to learn the skills you need to be the best possible parent you can be.

What if I told you that focusing more time and energy on your *own* well-being will directly benefit your child? This might sound counterintuitive, but it's true. Self-care in this context means, in part, learning to recognize the impact your child's behavioral problems have on your physical and mental health. We cannot give what we do not have. If we're coming from a place of frustration and feeling emotionally overwhelmed (understandably so), then we can't effectively model things like self-compassion, empathy, patience, and consistency. These are all vital behaviors your child will need to learn in order to more effectively manage their powerful emotions.

This book is going to ask you to do something that may feel radical, which is to put *yourself* first. You may be thinking, *Who has time for that?* or *I bought this book because my* kid *needs help!* I understand that things may seem desperate and out of control right now. You probably feel scared of what will happen if you can't get things "under control" soon. Your feelings are valid, but I invite you to take a step back and view your challenges from a different perspective. Understanding how your emotions are impacted by your child's behavior is essential to breaking the difficult pattern you and your child are stuck in.

How This Book Is Different

This book differs from others on ODD because of its two-pronged approach: It addresses your own need for self-care, coping skills, and parenting tools as well as your child's need for better emotion regulation and coping skills. The first part of this book will walk you through how to put on your own "oxygen mask" of skills and practices, while the second part is a behavior-change program to help reduce your child's oppositional behaviors. Critically, you must recognize and start to meet your own needs *first*, before you'll be ready to implement the program—so please don't skip to part two.

In part one, you'll learn about the many ways your child's behavior impacts how you feel, think, and react to them and to your whole family. The goal of this part of the book is to help you regain a sense of confidence in your role as a parent, understand patterns that have emerged in your relationship with your ODD child, and learn about the ways those patterns may be undermining your parenting goals. It will also provide tools to help you respond to your child with greater calm and more focused intention. I'll teach you healthy and practical communication tactics, mindfulness practices, and coping strategies to prepare you for part two of this book—taking care of your child.

Part two focuses on strategies to help your child learn new skills to manage their intense feelings, thoughts, and behaviors. This section will educate you on the function of your child's defiant behaviors and how you might be inadvertently reinforcing them. Next come the meat and potatoes of this treatment protocol: a detailed plan for systematically implementing alternative behaviors, clear and consistent boundaries, and effective consequences.

All the strategies and tools I'm offering here have been tested and shown to be highly effective in addressing a range of behavioral challenges. I've tailored them to be as practical and efficient as possible, because I understand behavior change is hard work and the best skills are those that are readily used. My goal is to make this book as user-friendly as possible so that you'll be able to implement the strategies even in moments of high stress. Many of the exercises included in the book are designed to help you work collaboratively with your child on ways to move forward. Though this program is full of tools to help your child make lasting changes, it's also likely that you or your child will need the help of a therapist or other specialist if the behaviors persist or become more extreme. If you feel you need extra support now, look into available services in your area.

What Do I Need to Get Started?

The most important thing you need to get started on this program is a giant dose of hope! I know that sounds corny, but I really mean it. Children have an amazing capacity for change. With the right guidance, your child can replace their challenging behaviors with healthy, appropriate, effective life skills.

I encourage you to take your time reading each chapter. This is a marathon, not a sprint. The goal is not to merely finish reading the book but to begin integrating the skills it teaches into your daily life. You may be tempted to hurry through part one, but try to spend a while getting a good handle on the tools. Remember, if you neglect your own needs, you will be less effective in helping your child.

You will need some materials to complete the exercises. I recommend getting a notebook that you use solely for this work. You may also want to use it to journal your progress. A day planner or calendar can be helpful for scheduling your self-care activities, setting time-limited goals, and marking milestones to gauge improvement. For the meditation exercises, having a quiet spot can be helpful. (Even a closet works.) Calming music, nature sounds, or guided-imagery apps make mindfulness skills easier. Once you have these, you're ready to get started!

Takeaways

- Parenting a child with ODD is emotionally difficult.
- Learning to care for your emotional well-being (part one) will have a direct impact on your ability to care for your child's (part two).
- Helping your child recover from ODD is a big undertaking. It necessitates a lot of effort, patience, consistency, and follow-through.
- This book was written to take the emotional needs of both you and your child into consideration.
- It's not how fast you read the book; it's how consistently and effectively you work the changes into your daily routine.

CHAPTER TWO

Be the Change You Want to See in Your Child

How Your Child's ODD Affects You

Parenting a child with ODD can take a toll on every aspect of your life. Since ODD is a problematic behavior pattern between children and the adults in their lives, it makes sense that parents would bear the brunt of ODD defiance. That's why taking care of yourself must be your first line of defense in treating ODD.

As I've said, the strain of caring for a child diagnosed with ODD can negatively impact your mental and physical health. Chronic stress can lead to many short- and long-term health consequences. You may find you're more susceptible to illness, struggle to maintain healthy eating, or have lower energy, further exacerbating the stress of daily life. And how's your mental health? Do you feel depressed or anxious? Studies consistently find that parents of children with behavioral disorders are at greater risk for developing mental health concerns. Anxiety and depression can greatly reduce your quality of life and make you feel hopeless. Additionally, trying to manage chronic stress can lead to an unhealthy reliance on things like overeating, alcohol, or other substances.

Your health impacts how you parent. Though depression also influences parenting practices, anxiety has been shown to be especially disruptive to parent-child relationships. Research by Kashdan, et al. (2004) revealed that parental anxiety is related to an increase in negative discipline (punishment), social distress, and controlling behaviors. It also decreased parental warmth and positive engagement, qualities that build connection in the critical parental bond. These things all have a negative impact on the parent-child relationship, intensifying disruptive behavior patterns and potentially leading to an increase in the child's aggression. In response, parents feel more stress and anxiety.

Parenting your child may also have occupational consequences. It can be challenging to find consistent care for a child struggling with ODD, but it's hard to leave work every time your child finds himself in the principal's office yet again. Childcare difficulties or work absences can impact your financial well-being and further exacerbate your stress.

ODD and Your Family

Due to the unpredictable and persistent nature of this disorder, living with a child with ODD can feel like walking on eggshells. Parents and siblings often develop routines intended to not "set off" the child— which may inadvertently help perpetuate the behaviors they're trying to avoid. Functionally, ODD turns the traditional family hierarchy on its head. Instead of the parents being at the top of the family system, the child's ODD behaviors run the show. This isn't because anyone, including the child, wants it to be this way; it's simply a by-product of the disorder. You may find that you've developed special rules for your child in an effort to reduce their acting out or enlisted your other children to help manage the ODD child's behavior. All of these are common means of trying to cope with an untenable situation, but they disrupt family routines, strain relationships, and increase everyone's stress.

That includes siblings. I often hear from parents that they know the disruption caused by the defiant child is unfair to their other kids, but they don't know how to prevent it. Other siblings can get lost in the shuffle when the problematic behavior of the ODD child drains so many parental resources. They may also be the victims of their sibling's aggression or threats, which can leave them frightened and anxious.

It's also hard to sustain a romantic relationship when both partners are under intense stress, and disagreeing about rules and consequences related to the ODD child's behavior can further increase that stress. If your partnership feels unsupportive, it can feed the vicious cycle of stress and problematic behavior.

ODD in School and Outside the Home

We live in a time of "zero tolerance" policies in schools, which makes the educational system precarious for children with ODD. Defiance in general isn't handled very effectively in most schools, and these children are at increased risk of suspension and even expulsion, especially as rules about bullying and aggression become stricter. School, with its rules and authority figures, can be triggering for these kids; add in the pressure of zero tolerance and school can feel like an emotional war zone.

Children with ODD don't always have difficulty outside the home. Some actually do quite well in other settings and exhibit their most disruptive behaviors only with their families. If this is the case, pay attention to what's different in those settings and what about those environments seems to be working for your child. For example, does your child do well in school because their teacher is firm, structured, and consistent? Collaborate with the other adults in your child's life; teachers, grandparents, tutors, and coaches can be essential sources of tools and strategies.

Does your child struggle in other settings as well? If so, notice what it is that sets them off. If it can't be avoided, work to prepare them for the situation ahead of time and get their feedback on what could make the experience easier for them. Collaboration can help them feel like they have a voice. ODD behavior can take over a household, but with work, you can loosen the grip that it has on your family.

Breaking the Cycle of Reactivity

In order to loosen ODD's grip on your family, you need a better understanding of what's driving your child's most difficult behaviors. Often, the worst acting out is not something your child is doing *to* you or others but rather a means by which they try to manage their own strong emotions.

The term *emotional reactivity* refers to intense emotional arousal, which can result in problematic behaviors in both kids and parents. In children with ODD, this cycle or pattern of reactivity is typically frequent and intense, including tantrums, screaming, and other extreme behaviors. The problem with emotional reactivity is that it's an unrestrained explosion of uncomfortable feelings. Though it serves the function of temporarily releasing the discomfort, it's rarely a helpful means of problem-solving.

Emotional reactivity is also contagious. When your child gets triggered, you can get triggered in response. Because as an adult you've had more years to learn useful coping strategies, you likely don't get triggered every single time they do, but when you do, it leaves its mark on your relationship and on your confidence as a parent.

The remedy? Mindfully, thoughtfully *responding* to the situation, rather than simply *reacting* to the difficult behavior in the moment. This may seem like semantics, but there is actually a huge difference between responding and reacting. Reaction is automatic, and very little thought or purpose goes into it. It's essentially a reflex that engages due to an external event or internal feeling (like anger). Responding, on the other hand, requires intent. It isn't automatic; it's a purposeful action based on your goals for the situation's outcome.

What Are Your Triggers?

So, how does one learn to respond to a child's emotional reactivity without getting sucked into a conflict? First, you must be able to identify the things that trigger you.

We all have triggers—those situations or emotions that can set us off in a split second. One of my biggest triggers as a parent is whining. When my son starts whining, all patience is immediately sucked out of my body, my ability to listen completely shuts off, and my empathy tank is drained. Am I likely to make good parenting choices when I'm feeling like that? The answer is a resounding no! I'm much more likely to speak without thinking or automatically reach for a negative consequence for my son before I have all the relevant facts.

An important first step in learning how to prevent this kind of situation is to identify which behaviors and events are most triggering for you, so you can face them with awareness when they arise. I once had a client who had huge blowouts with her ODD son every time they went to the grocery store. Her son was no more disobedient than usual during these outings, so she couldn't figure out why her patience was so short. Eventually she realized that her son would usually ask her to buy something that wasn't on her list, and because the family was on a tight budget, the request provoked feelings of guilt and made her feel like she wasn't adequately providing for her child. Had she not made the effort to understand her triggers, she might still think she was reacting in anger only because of her son's behavior, without recognizing her own role in the situation.

Let's use an exercise to identify the situations, behaviors, thoughts, and feelings that tend to set you off. As you work through it, consider if there are times of day that seem especially challenging or places you go with your child that always seem to result in a fight.

EXERCISE: Identifying Your Triggers

Understanding what makes you vulnerable to reacting to your child's behavior is important in reducing conflicts. This exercise is designed to help you identify your triggers.

Think about three situations in the last two weeks when you were triggered by your child's emotional reactivity. For each situation, answer the following questions in your notebook:

- What were you doing *just before* you were triggered?
- Where were you? What time was it?
- Who else was there in the triggering situation?

- What did you do when triggered (e.g., shouting, making threats)?
- What purpose did your eruption serve in that moment (e.g., released tension, ended child's tantrum)?

Note: If you find yourself stuck trying to figure out what triggered you, consider your mood at the time (anxious, frustrated), physical condition (headache, hungry, tired), and the thoughts you were having (*I'm so sick of this!*).

Now, consider the pros and cons of how you handled each triggering situation. What went well? What were any negative consequences? In your notebook, jot down both pros and cons for each of the three situations. If you're having trouble finding the pros, just remember that all behavior serves a purpose. For example, if you yelled at your daughter when she refused to get out of the car for school, and she exited as a result, the pro was that it worked, while the con was you felt bad for losing your temper or that it didn't prevent her from refusing to get out of the car the next day. Remember, this is not an exercise in judging yourself. Rather, the goal is to understand your own behavior patterns as you relate to your child.

Alternatives to Conflict

Once you've started to look for your triggers, you'll begin to notice them more readily. However, just understanding what triggers you isn't enough to make the changes you're seeking. Effective trigger management requires some behavior changes on your part. This is not intended to scare you off but rather to validate how difficult it may feel at first to try to respond differently when triggered.

"Taking five" is a strategy I teach my clients to help them manage their triggers. It's literally taking a break to temporarily get yourself out of an overwhelming situation. I've had more than one parent tell me the bathroom can be a safe haven when they need to pull it together.

Goal Setting for the Parent-Child Relationship

ODD affects the parent-child relationship in many ways. From a parent's standpoint, being emotionally open to someone who consistently hurts you is challenging, which creates a complicated bond between you and your youngster. Part of learning to manage your child's ODD is intentionally building a healthy relationship with them, despite their struggles.

The following exercise will require you to do some reflecting and goal setting, so dedicate at least 30 minutes to it. If you need more time, come back to it later.

Write your responses to the following prompts in your notebook:

Miracle question: Pretend you wake up tomorrow and a miracle has occurred. Your child's ODD symptoms are completely gone! What will be different? How will your relationship be different? What types of things will you do together? How will it feel being around your child?

What to do today: Now that you've identified how your relationship would be different if your child were symptom-free, create two relationship goals you'd like to work on over the next week that could get you closer to the relationship you're seeking. For example, if you and your child played soccer together in the "miracle" scenario, then invite them to play soccer this weekend. If you imagined that you and your child would talk more openly about hard things, you could share a minor problem that you're experiencing and ask for feedback. Write down the two short-term relationship goals you can work on now to help move you toward your larger relationship goals.

Strong relationships evolve over time. Once you've accomplished the two small goals, make new ones for next week and the week after. Continue to write them in your notebook to help you keep track of your relationship progress.

Simply checking in with how you're feeling, especially in situations you know trigger you, is also really helpful. You can't reduce emotional reactivity if you don't monitor your emotions. Start building the practice of paying attention to your feelings and how intense they are moment to moment. When you're more than moderately frustrated, try some deep breathing, take a walk, or do something else that helps you cope.

Think of the times you've given in to your emotions as useful information on what *not* to do next time. If you lost your cool while making dinner because your son refused to set the table, what did you learn from the experience? Do you find you're more likely to fire back when rushed? Or do you put too much pressure on yourself to get everything done? If so, what is one thing you can do differently next time, knowing this is a liability? Perhaps it's having cereal or another ready-made meal on certain nights. Try that thing out, and see how it goes.

The Power of Mindfulness

Mindfulness is a powerful tool for coping with the kind of difficult emotions that frequently come up for parents trying to manage a defiant child. Mindfulness practice trains you to be aware of what's happening or what you're feeling in the moment, without judging that experience or struggling against it. The skills that mindfulness teaches—nonreactivity, staying grounded in your present experience—will help you be a better parent to your ODD child and stay calm even when they're acting out.

Remember, when working with a child, the change must begin with you—and mindfulness is a great place to start. Many people mistakenly believe that mindfulness is about zoning out or falling into a meditative trance. Instead, it's about fully embracing your current state, even when that's uncomfortable. Our society as a whole goes to great lengths to avoid experiencing the present (drinking, overscheduling, social media). I like to think of mindfulness as a way of going back to basics.

Building your mindfulness skills involves intentionally engaging with your experience in the moment and training yourself not to immediately react to inner experiences like anger or frustration. Another key factor is learning not to judge your thoughts, feelings, or experiences, because once you do, suddenly the here and now becomes something you have to change or "fix." Mindfulness is the antidote to that, as it teaches us simply to notice and observe our experiences, rather than judging or struggling with them.

Present-Moment Awareness

In his book *The Mindful Brain*, Daniel Siegel explains, "Mindful awareness . . . actually involves more than just simply being aware: It involves being aware of aspects of the mind itself. Instead of being on automatic and mindless, mindfulness helps us awaken, and by reflecting on the mind we are enabled to make choices and thus change becomes possible." How does being aware of the present moment lead to change? Put simply, learning to stay in the moment, rather than avoiding it, increases our ability to tolerate distress, manage our emotions, and more successfully problem-solve, because we're cultivating a calmer, more focused state of mind.

Interestingly, according to a 2010 Harvard study by Killingsworth and Gilbert, when people focus on the present moment, they're more likely to report an improvement in mood, even when the present moment involves something irritating like waiting in line or sitting in a meeting. Generally speaking, we feel better when we're fully present and engaged, and from a behavior-change standpoint it's relatively easy compared to, say, getting a new job. This improvement can help give you the emotional energy to help your child manage their ODD symptoms more effectively.

MEDITATION: Noting Thoughts and Stories

This meditation will help you focus on the present and become more aware of your thoughts.

Spend one minute focusing on your breath. Breathe in deeply through your nose, and slowly exhale through your mouth. When your mind wanders, redirect your focus to your breath.

Now, continue your breathing and pay attention to any thoughts that arise. Imagine that you're an observer of the thought, noticing its distinct characteristics. Does it have a color? Is it dark or light?

You don't need to make any changes to the thought. It's neither good nor bad. It just is. Does it have weight? Is it heavy or featherlight? If you notice yourself judging the experience, imagine that judgment turning into vapor and floating off into the distance. Refocus your attention on being an observer.

Is the thought pulling you to the future or the past? Simply notice what's going on right now. Allow curiosity to flow through you. Other thoughts may come in; it's okay to let them be. Thoughts pass by like bubbles floating in the breeze.

Are your thoughts starting to weave a story? Notice the tone and shape of the story without trying to rewrite it. See the words of the story gently roll past you like a ribbon of letters.

Let yourself observe the stream of thoughts, words, and stories until you're ready to focus on your breathing. Let them fade away gently as you breathe in deeply and then slowly breathe out until your lungs feel empty.

Now, focus on your breath for one minute, paying attention to each inhale and exhale.

Practice this as part of your self-care routine.

Take a Pause

As a parent, I know finding time to introduce a pause or break into your already overscheduled day may seem like another task on your to-do list. Still, it's important, because it allows you the mental and emotional space to attend to your needs, even in emotionally charged situations. Though it's beneficial to make this a daily practice, it's particularly helpful in tense situations with your child.

Taking a pause means intentionally taking a break from the situation at hand, and it's a major tool in managing reactivity. It gives you far more options than simply reacting in the moment. Just as you may suggest to your child that they take a break, you have the right to use this tool as well. When a conflict is escalating, if possible, try walking away for two minutes to give yourself some time to breathe and calm down.

Practice it first when you're not stressed, so it's easier to use when you are. A simple way to weave it into your routine is to take two minutes to focus on your breathing before you start your morning regimen. The better you get, the more likely you'll be to use it when you need it.

When taking a pause, make sure to focus on things that can help you de-escalate. The point is to calm down a bit—replaying the frustrating incident in your head won't do that! Instead, do deep breathing, and try to narrow your attention to things you can see, hear, smell, touch, or taste. These are all mindfulness skills aimed at increasing your sense of well-being and reducing the likelihood that you'll be reactive. Fortunately, learning to pause doesn't need to take a lot of time—just consistency.

The Power of Compassion

The purpose of this chapter is to help you begin to make the changes you want to see in your child. At the heart of this work is the need for compassion—for you and for your child. Compassion is a powerful tool that can lead to remarkable changes in parents and children. In fact, psychologist Paul Gilbert founded a whole model of psychotherapy called compassion-focused therapy (CFT), based on building compassion for oneself and others as a means to reduce suffering. Studies by Judge (2012) and Sommers-Spijkerman (2018) have shown CFT to be highly effective in reducing distress levels, self-criticism, shame, and anxiety.

Let's take a closer look at what compassion looks like in action and how it applies to the work you want to do with your child.

Self-Compassion

Self-compassion is the ability to feel sympathetic to your own pain and struggle, *especially* when you believe you've failed. Watching your child struggle with ODD can be heartbreaking and anxiety-inducing, and unsuccessful attempts to help your child can create feelings of hopelessness and inadequacy. It's not uncommon for parents to have thoughts like *How did I let things get this bad?* or *Where did I go wrong?* For many caregivers, keeping their own emotions contained when a child is acting out can seem impossible. As a result, self-blame, shame, and guilt are common in families with ODD kids. In addition to the emotional distress these feelings cause, focusing too intently on them can get you stuck. It's impossible to become a more confident parent by making yourself feel *worse*. The fix? A healthy dose of self-compassion.

Cultivating self-compassion can be a big part of helping your child overcome ODD, because it teaches us empathy, acceptance, resilience, and accountability. The more we can accept the parts of ourselves we're not so fond of, the more we practice forgiving ourselves for our all-too-human failings, and the more tolerance and compassion we can feel for others, including our children. The goal is to start where you are: as an imperfect parent of an imperfect child in an imperfect world. The lens of self-compassion lets us see our mistakes both as aspects of being human and as opportunities for growth.

Self-Compassion

The following meditation will help you cultivate feelings of self-compassion. Remember, the more you grow your self-compassion, the more compassion you'll have for your child.

Spend one minute focusing on your breath. Inhale deeply through your nose, and slowly exhale through your mouth.

Imagine a small, glowing ball floating in front of you. Notice how it softly emits light. The ball has a golden label that reads *Self-Compassion.*

Reach out and take hold of the ball. Once it's in your hands, feel its warmth spread through your body. Notice the warmth in your chest and your heart. Feel it radiate down to your toes and up to the top of your head. Enjoy the calming feeling it brings.

Now, think back to a time when someone showed you compassion. Remember how it felt to know they cared, to feel loved and accepted. Recall the comfort of knowing you weren't alone. Imagine that person handing you the glowing ball. Hold it for as long as you'd like.

Think of a time when you needed compassion. What did you feel or think? Imagine taking hold of the glowing ball once again and turning the compassion toward yourself. Breathe it in. Feel the warmth and comfort. Notice your thoughts and feelings as you allow self-compassion to sweep over you. Sit with this for a moment.

Observe the thoughts, feelings, and physical sensations that arise as you bask in the warmth of your self-compassion.

When you're ready, take five deep breaths and open your eyes. Whenever you feel like you need some grace, recall the golden ball and how it felt to embrace self-compassion.

Compassion for Your Child

Children with highly explosive, defiant behaviors are in pain, even as they cause pain to others. I've never met a child who enjoys getting in trouble or acting out. Their oppositional behavior isn't due to some character flaw; they're simply lacking the tools to effectively cope with intense emotions. If they knew a better way to manage, they would.

In her parenting guide *Child-Wise*, Cathy Rindner Tempelsman notes, "The child who acts unlovable is the child who most needs to be loved." Working to view challenging behaviors from the perspective of compassion will impact how you respond to your child's outbursts. If you start with the premise that your child is doing their best, it allows you to see their struggle instead of their defiance and creates space for focusing on solutions rather than problems. Modeling understanding and warmth will also help your child learn to cultivate their own supply of self-compassion.

EXERCISE: How Are You Feeling?

The following is a self-assessment to check for symptoms of depression or anxiety. Both are common in parents of children with ODD, and I want to be sure your needs are being met. Write down your responses in your notebook, along with today's date. (You'll do this self-assessment again in chapter 8.)

Part A
1. Have you felt down or sad lately?
2. Do you find it hard to enjoy things you usually like?
3. Any changes in weight or appetite recently?
4. Are you sleeping too little or too much?
5. Do you feel tired or fatigued often?

6. Do you frequently experience feelings of worthlessness and/or guilt?
7. Has it become hard to make decisions?
8. Do you feel that things in your life are hopeless?
9. Is it difficult to think or focus?
10. Any suicidal thoughts or thoughts of dying?*

Five or more "yes" responses indicate you're likely experiencing depressive symptoms. Talk to your physician about your symptoms, and consider if therapy is right for you.

*If you answered yes to question 10, please seek professional help immediately. If you aren't able to keep yourself and your family safe, please call 911 or go to your nearest emergency room.

Part B

1. Do you have high levels of anxiety?
2. Are you worrying more than usual?
3. Is it hard to manage your worries?
4. Are you feeling restless or tense?
5. Do you get tired easily?
6. Is concentrating difficult?
7. Does your mind go blank often?
8. Are you more irritable than usual?
9. Do you have muscle tension?
10. Have you had sleep difficulties like trouble falling or staying asleep?

If you answered yes to questions 1 and 2 *and* three or more others, you're likely experiencing anxiety symptoms. Talking to your physician or a therapist could be a helpful next step.

Takeaways

- Your child's ODD symptoms impact everyone in the family.
- Breaking the cycle of emotional volatility is possible!
- Identifying your triggers is the first step in helping your child learn to manage their intense feelings.
- Mindfulness—the practice of embracing the present in an open, nonjudgmental way—helps improve mood and manage intense emotions.
- Self-compassion increases compassion for your child.
- Checking in on how you're doing is part of this work.
- If you're experiencing depression and anxiety symptoms, especially suicidal thoughts or intent, please seek professional help immediately, including, if needed, calling 911 or going to your nearest emergency room.

CHAPTER THREE

Managing Difficult Emotions

Facing Discomfort

Picture this: It's a beautiful summer morning, and you're taking the kids to the beach for the day. You've gotten up early to pack sunblock and towels. The kids are still asleep, and all is quiet in the house, but instead of feeling excited about the outing, you find yourself feeling anxious, tense, and even frustrated. Thoughts of your defiant child starting arguments in the car or having a meltdown over the smallest request flash through your mind. You remember the last time you attempted a family trip to the beach and had to turn around before you got there because he had a violent tantrum. Your anxiety and frustration then turn to guilt, maybe even shame. You tell yourself that today may be different. Still, you can't shake your negative mood, and your worries persist. Does this sound familiar? This is the reality for most families living with ODD.

Do you remember the terms *hypervigilance* and *trigger* we discussed in chapter 1? Your brain has been programmed through repeated experiences with your ODD child to anticipate the worst. You're not feeling on edge around your kid because you *want* to—your brain is just trying to keep you safe by anticipating problems. Your child's prickly behavior has likely become a huge wedge in your relationship. Parents I work with often report painful, conflicted feelings about their ODD child. Facing the discomfort of these difficult feelings, and learning how to act calmly even when you're feeling them, is an important part of making progress.

Anger, Sadness, Fear, and Shame

You might feel the urge to skip past this section. Who wants to dwell on anger, sadness, fear, or shame? But understanding how these emotions impact you and your relationships is crucial.

First, I want to emphasize that all your negative feelings are totally normal. They're valid reactions to the situation you're in, and it's okay to feel them. I'd also encourage you to take a closer look at some of your most potent emotions, like anger, and see what else is lurking within them. As it turns out, *sadness* is often the driving force behind anger and guilt; we often prefer to avoid the vulnerability of sadness by covering it over with a secondary emotion. As unpleasant as anger may be, it feels more powerful to be mad than to be sad—but the sense of control it provides rarely lasts. I'm willing to bet that a lot of your anger at your ODD child stems from sadness for your child's struggle and fear for their future.

Parents also report feeling guilt and shame when talking about their feelings toward their defiant child. Both emotions are understandable, but guilt, though painful, is far more useful than shame. In proper doses, guilt allows you to see how you may have inadvertently contributed to your child's behavior problems. If correctly channeled, it can lead to problem-solving and to changing your own behavior. Shame, on the other hand, is usually toxic. Shame will tell you you're a bad parent and the reason your child is acting out. Rather than motivating you the way guilt can, shame often keeps parents from seeking the help they need.

We've established that parenting an ODD child means you're dealing with a lot of strong, unpleasant emotions. We also know, because you're reading this book, that you're determined to make progress with your child despite the pain or anxiety you're feeling. One helpful step toward progress lies in changing not how we feel but rather our *relationship to* our most difficult feelings. Strategies including mindfulness, acceptance and commitment therapy (ACT), and cognitive behavioral therapy (CBT) are especially useful here. Mindfulness practices can be particularly helpful in creating some distance between us and our strongest emotions. Opening a small gap between having the initial feeling— say, anger—and acting on it can help us keep our cool even in difficult situations.

MEDITATION: Observing
Your Emotions and Thoughts

Set aside five minutes in a quiet, comfortable place. Set a timer or
your phone alarm.

Take one minute and focus entirely on deep breathing. Breathe in
deeply through your nose, and slowly release through your mouth.
Your in breaths should be so deep that it feels like your abdomen is
expanding, only to be reduced on your out breaths. When you notice
your attention wandering, refocus on your breathing.

Close your eyes, and for two minutes focus entirely on what emotions you're experiencing. Let your body give you clues, if needed.
If you can't pinpoint the feeling(s), just notice if you're comfortable
or uncomfortable.

Now, imagine a beautiful blue sky with puffy white clouds and a
gentle breeze blowing them past. Picture yourself carefully placing
each emotion you're feeling onto the passing clouds.

Notice how the clouds float past you with the breeze. First they
were right in front of you, and now they're gone in the distance.
If some clouds stay for a while, let them be. The wind will ease them
away soon.

If you find yourself judging the feeling or becoming distracted,
focus on the fluffy clouds and the gentle breeze.

Next, do the same with your thoughts for two minutes.

Place all the words and sentences running through your mind onto
the clouds. No matter how distracting or distressing, let the thought
clouds float past. Remember, they're just thoughts and have no power
in themselves. You can notice what they look and feel like without
doing anything about them. You can just let them float past.

If they become stuck, or you begin to judge them, that's normal.
Just let them be until they're ready to float past.

When the timer sounds, take five deep breaths to end the
meditation.

The Avoidance Trap

Avoidance—the attempt to dodge and/or suppress painful feelings, thoughts, and situations—is enticing. It's a natural human response to pain and distress, and it promises comfort in the face of discomfort. Unfortunately, the more we avoid the things that trigger difficult emotions, the more overwhelming those things become, which only motivates us to avoid them more. And when your child is the source of your discomfort, avoidance can greatly undermine your parenting and your child's potential for growth and change. The goal of healthy coping is not to push away the inevitable difficulties that arise in life but to tolerate and accept them—and move forward despite their presence.

Avoidance can show up in all sorts of ways and isn't always as obvious as physically avoiding whatever's distressing you (by, for example, sending your defiant child to their room when things get heated). Here are some common ways I've seen avoidance play out in the families of ODD kids.

Resignation/despair: By the time families come to my office, they're often highly discouraged. Parents will report, "There's no hope," "Nothing works," or, "I cannot do any more than I'm already doing." Clinging to resignation may help you avoid fear and sadness, but it offers no hope for change.

Placating/giving in: Tired of big meltdowns? I don't blame you. Unfortunately, giving in to your defiant child in an attempt to avoid blowouts only reinforces their unruly behaviors. Commonly, this form of avoidance manifests itself in inconsistency—e.g., not following through with stated consequences or inadvertently rewarding inappropriate behaviors to keep the peace.

Excessive control/punishment: Some parents try to avoid the discomfort of their child's behavior by inflicting punishment and control.

Their intention is usually to help the child behave appropriately through strict rules, with harsh punishments to enforce compliance. While structure is necessary for ODD kids, this avoidance strategy often backfires because it prevents the child from feeling capable of succeeding and creates unnecessary friction.

Justification/blame: Another common avoidance strategy is making excuses or blaming others for a defiant child's behavior ("she was too tired," "the teacher was really hard on him"). Emotionally, this allows the parent to avoid seeing the child as "bad," but it also splits the child into "good" and "bad" parts when they're really a whole being with complex needs.

Separation/disconnecting: Psychologically, it's challenging to be emotionally connected to an ODD kid who is simultaneously lovable and frightening. Parents might try to avoid that challenge by separating themselves emotionally from their child. I often hear parents say, "I just can't connect with him," "I love her, but I don't like her," or, "I don't feel the same about him as I do my other children." These parents love their children very much, but they're also overwhelmed, and sometimes they build avoidant psychological defenses against that.

Anger: Parents who live with the daily struggle of caring for a defiant child often develop a thick skin of anger to avoid feelings of sadness and fear. The developmental trajectory of a defiant child is frightening and painful, especially without intervention. Because anger allows us to feel less vulnerable than fear and pain, it can seem like a welcome relief. Unfortunately, it does little to actually solve the problems ODD presents.

Though these avoidance strategies may offer short-term comfort, in the long run they only cause more distress by perpetuating unhealthy behavior patterns instead of facing them head-on and solving them.

Getting Unstuck

Now that we've reviewed the most common avoidance traps, it's time to start learning how to get out of them. Getting unstuck means, first of all, acknowledging that you're currently stuck. Since you're reading this book, you probably recognize you need some help shaking loose from the unhelpful behavior patterns you're caught in with your child.

Of the avoidance traps described above, which ones best describe your situation? Now is the time to take an honest look at how your actions are contributing to your child's defiance. I say that not to place blame or shame but rather to provide a starting place for transformation. Since we can change only the things we acknowledge, I encourage you to be as candid as possible when it comes to identifying your stuck points. Do you find yourself disconnecting from your child when overwhelmed? Is giving in to their tantrums easier than holding your ground? Does your anger get out of control, leaving you feeling ashamed and guilty?

Recognizing these things is hard—but not as hard as remaining stuck. You have more power to change this situation than you think.

WRITTEN EXERCISE: A Letter to Your Child

The following exercise is intended to help you express your feelings toward your child in an open, honest, and safe way. You will *not* give the letter to your child; rather it's an opportunity for you to acknowledge the impact that your child's behavior has had on you and the hopes and dreams you still have for them.

In your notebook, write a letter to your child, **which will not be delivered**, by answering the following prompts:

- When you were born, these were my hopes and dreams for you.
- This is what I love about you. (List qualities you admire and reasons you love your child.)

- These are my hopes for you in the future. (What do you want most for them?)
- This is how your words, actions, and attitude have made me feel about myself and about you. (Be as honest as possible, even though it may be very painful.)
- This is the impact that your behavior and ODD symptoms have had on my life. (Include the influence on your other relationships, career, well-being, beliefs, and goals.)
- These are the ways I've tried to cope. (Note helpful and unhelpful coping skills you've tried.)
- These are the uncomfortable thoughts, feelings, and situations I've tried to avoid in order to manage the impact of your actions on me. (List avoidance strategies used.)
- This is why I still feel hopeful. (If you're reading this, then there's at least a bit of hope—what is it?)

Once you've written the letter, you may wish to shred it or put it away somewhere safe. The purpose of the letter is to express your pain and acknowledge the impact ODD has had on you so you can move forward to the next phase of this work.

The Power of Acceptance

We've talked a lot about avoidance and why we tend to run away from difficult thoughts, feelings, and situations. If you're like most people, you might be asking yourself what you're supposed to do with the discomfort you're feeling. After all, if you can't avoid it, then you're just stuck with it, right? Wrong. The key is acceptance. In psychological terms, *acceptance* means allowing yourself to experience thoughts, emotions, or situations without trying to change them or push them away.

In their book *Acceptance and Commitment Therapy*, Steven Hayes, Kirk Strosahl, and Kelly Wilson define acceptance as requiring both *behavioral willingness* and *psychological acceptance*. Behavioral willingness is a voluntary choice to be present with all the thoughts, feelings, and experiences that arise in life—even the painful ones. You can intentionally choose to remain present in your life, no matter how challenging that may be at times, in service of things you value, like closeness with your child. Psychological acceptance is "the adoption of an intentionally open, receptive, flexible, and nonjudgmental posture with respect to moment-to-moment experience." Again, acceptance is a deliberate, conscious process intended to cultivate flexibility, tolerance, and eventually self-acceptance.

I liken the acceptance process to a game of tug-of-war where you're on one end of the rope and the painful feeling, thought, or experience is on the other. The more you pull, the harder your opponent pulls in response. Psychologically, this means that the more effort you put into resisting the experience, the greater the intensity, duration, and frequency of that experience in your life. In this metaphor, acceptance means *letting go of the rope*. When you do that, the fight between you and the distressing situation ceases, because you're no longer participating in the battle.

Properly practiced, acceptance helps you grow more comfortable with your discomfort. I know that sounds paradoxical, but it works. Bottling up negative thoughts and feelings can lead to depression, anxiety, health problems, and unhelpful coping strategies, which only fuel your distress. Acceptance is the best, most realistic way to meet your emotional challenges in a healthy way. Life is full of distressing events, from small disappointments to heartbreaking losses. Since there's no way to avoid them, the best way through is to accept their presence as part of life—and learn to move forward anyway.

I want to take a moment to differentiate between acceptance and giving up. In ACT, acceptance is *not* about giving up; rather, it's a highly active and intentional process. Acceptance is far harder to do than the passive process of resigning yourself to negative thoughts, feelings, and experiences, because it requires persistence and a commitment to your values and aspirations.

MEDITATION: Inviting Difficult Emotions

This meditation will help you work on your ability to tolerate distressing feelings. It's a safe, structured way to practice becoming comfortable with discomfort.

At the end of the day, set aside 10 minutes in a quiet, comfortable place. Set an alarm if you wish.

Take one minute and focus entirely on deep breathing. Breathe in deeply through your nose, and slowly release through your mouth. Your in breathing should be deep enough that you feel your abdomen expanding when you inhale.

If you notice your attention wandering, refocus on your breathing.

Close your eyes and consider all the things that happened to you today from the time you woke up until this very moment. Let all the highs and lows pass through your consciousness.

Now, think of the hardest part of your day. Notice the thoughts and feelings that arise as you recall this difficult experience. Are they comfortable or uncomfortable? If you notice yourself resisting any thoughts or feelings, try to just sit with them as they are.

Notice your body as you remember this hard point in your day. From the top of your head down to your toes, recognize any sensations you may be experiencing, including warmth, tension, or pain. Allow these feelings to be.

Take five deep breaths in through your nose, slowly exhaling through your mouth.

Imagine yourself gently picking up the difficult feelings from today's challenging experience. Imagine them in the palm of your hand. Notice how they look and feel, the weight of them. See them from all angles.

If you notice you're becoming distracted, just return your attention to the feelings. When you're done, imagine placing the feelings gently beside you.

It is now time to get a better look at your thoughts about today's difficulty. Imagine them as a slow stream of words flowing past you like the breeze. See each letter; note the size and color of the font. See them as they are: a collection of words strung together. Let them swirl around you until they're just letters.

Take five deep breaths and envision all of your painful, difficult thoughts, feelings, and physical sensations before you. Really see them in full detail. Let them know that they are valid.

Now, visualize yourself in the midst of this discomfort and remind yourself that you are strong enough to hold these hard things.

Take five last deep breaths and slowly open your eyes. How do you feel? What are you noticing?

Turning toward Pain

How do we learn to accept distress when our brains are pro-grammed to avoid painful things? The first step is to practice turning toward the pain we would normally try to suppress or work around. Every day you experience a whole range of emotions, whether you're aware of them all or not. You may feel irritated in traffic, then anxious about a big conference call, then excited about dinner plans. Feelings, and the thoughts that accompany them, come and go constantly.

It's human nature to push away what's negative, but while this might offer you short-term relief, it's not a remedy for pain. Instead, it exacerbates it. But when you consciously choose to lean in to your painful feelings, you're focusing on what's happening in the present moment instead of resisting reality.

Are you willing to learn to accept the pain as a means of moving past it? ACT focuses on living in line with your values and being committed to actions that support those values, no matter how you're feeling from moment to moment. For you, this may look like being open to the pain of seeing your child struggle while still being engaged with them because you value your relationship. It could also allow for you to have more self-acceptance rather than self-criticism and doubt. Turning toward discomfort is initially very challenging, but it becomes easier with practice.

Moving Forward Despite Challenges

In working toward long-term, sustainable changes for you and your child, you're taking on a huge challenge. The journey won't always be smooth. You'll stumble and perhaps at times fall. If that happens, remember: This work is hard because it matters—a lot. Helping your child make gains requires new skills, for them and for you. It also requires changes on your part that may seem counterintuitive or uncomfortably different from your usual MO. Be gentle with yourself as you go through this process. The goal is not perfection but persistence. Bumps in the road give you information about what areas need more time or work. There's no need to rush. The more time you allow for new habits to form, the greater the likelihood that you'll carry them into the future.

WRITTEN EXERCISE: Acceptance

"Why does my son get so angry?" "Why can't I get through to my daughter?" "Why is life so hard?!" Asking *why* questions can keep us stuck, because they focus our attention on how we think things *ought* to be rather than on reality.

In your notebook, make a list of 10 *why* questions that you often ask about yourself, your child, or challenging situations. Then go back and rewrite them, changing them from questions into statements. For example, "Why can't I get through to her?" could be revised to, "I can't get through to her." "Why is life so hard?" might become, "Life is so hard." The goal is to help you refocus your thoughts on the present and see and accept things as they are in the moment, rather than judging them.

Action Plan: Self-Care

Self-care is an essential element of well-being. Taking care of yourself isn't selfish—it's a prerequisite for caring for others. I like to think of self-care as a discipline, something to be practiced, like dance or painting. If you're like most parents I work with, you're probably thinking, *I don't have time for that*. I get it. You're incredibly busy and stressed by life's demands. But taking time to nurture yourself is essential. You can't get water from a dry well; self-care is how you fill yourself back up.

Create a self-care plan for the next seven days. Think for a minute about things that nourish or soothe you. They don't need to be elaborate activities. They should be simple enough that you'll actually do them.

In your notebook or planner, schedule one self-care activity each day. It's important to write your intentions down, because we tend to commit more to a task that we've set down in writing. Here are some suggestions to get you started. Don't be afraid to mix it up!

Meditations or guided imagery: Research shows the effectiveness of mediations and guided imagery as a means of increasing positive mood. There are countless meditation scripts available on Pinterest and YouTube. Keep these to 10 minutes or less.

Mindfulness: This is the practice of being aware of the present moment. A popular mindfulness activity: Take two minutes to notice five things you see, four things you hear, three things you can touch, two things you can smell, and one thing you can taste. This helps ground you in the present moment.

Exercise: Exercise is important for your physical and mental health. It releases endorphins that help improve mood, relieve stress, and reduce mild depression and anxiety symptoms. You don't need to exercise super hard or long; a 15-minute walk or stretch session will do.

Gratitude: Practicing gratitude has been shown to increase positive emotion. Try listing three things you're thankful for each day, or make a "gratitude jar" where you can drop in a daily note of gratitude for something or someone.

Quality time: Spending time with those you care about—or even a family pet—is a great way to refill your well. Just be sure that you're present, not tuning out by staring at your phone or the television.

Takeaways

- Facing uncomfortable feelings and thoughts is a necessary part of this work.
- Anger, sadness, anxiety, guilt, and shame are common, natural feelings for parents struggling to help their child with ODD.
- Avoidance of painful feelings, thoughts, and situations only makes them worse.
- Acceptance is the practice of allowing room for distressing emotions and thoughts without trying to change or get rid of them.
- Acceptance is an active process.
- Self-care is necessary, not selfish. You can't give back to others if you have nothing left in your own well.
- Self-care is a discipline that takes time and practice to become consistent.

CHAPTER FOUR

Mindful Communication

What Is Mindful Communication?

If you're like most parents raising a child with ODD, you and your child have a pattern—a habitual, entrenched way of communicating. You probably find yourself endlessly repeating phrases like "because I said so" or "don't make me tell you again!" But over time, these phrases lose their meaning. How can you break those patterns and express yourself in more constructive ways while also really listening to your child? The answer is mindful communication.

The simplest definition of mindful communication is that it's the exact opposite of *mindless* communication. It's not speaking reactively, or because you feel angry, or just to prove you're right. The goal is not only to speak but also to truly hear the person you're communicating with and respond to what they're saying. Listening is just as important as speaking—sometimes more so. And remember, communication is not just spoken words—it's also facial expressions, body movements, vocal tone/volume, and more.

Mindful communication is an intentional, active process. It requires present-moment awareness—checking in with your thoughts, feelings, and reactions—no matter how uncomfortable the conversation is, to stay committed to the goal of the conversation without falling into emotional reactivity. When you pay attention to how your emotions impact your communication style during an interaction, you can use that information to guide your next steps. For example, if you know you get cranky when you're frustrated, you might take a pause when you find yourself in a frustrating exchange with your child. If you notice that you tend to disengage when stressed, then do some mindfulness exercises before picking up your child from school. I find it helpful to check in with myself and ask, *Am I trying to win, or am I trying to find a solution?* If I'm trying to win, I know I'm not communicating effectively.

Let's take a closer look at how mindful communication can help your relationship with your child.

Mindful Communication and Your ODD Child

One of the hallmarks of ODD is argumentativeness. Your child probably has some major deficits in communication skills and falls back on argument and defiance when faced with a challenge. Mindful communication can give kids with ODD the skills they're lacking most: respectfulness, listening, empathy, and nonviolent communication.

One challenge in trying to communicate with your defiant child is that these kids can be explosive, escalating a conflict from 0 to 100 and leaving you feeling blindsided and defensive. It will take time, but by modeling mindful communication skills for your child, you'll teach them that you're no longer reacting to their eruptions in the same way, and they'll change how they respond to you. This is a first step in breaking those old, unhelpful communication patterns.

Respect is a foundational principle of mindful communication. Unfortunately, most families with an ODD child fall into a pattern of disrespectful interactions because of the inherent power struggle associated with defiance. You can model respect by being kind and courteous in your conversations—no yelling, sarcasm, or insults. Monitor your volume and tone. Talk to them like you would a colleague or friend. It doesn't have to be formal, but it should be polite. For example, if you'd like them to clean their room, "Please have your room straightened up, nothing on the floor, and toys put away before twelve o'clock," is much more respectful than, "Get your butt up and clean your room, now!" Remember, your child is a person and deserves kindness, regardless of how much they're acting out. By modeling respectful behavior, even in tough situations, you're demonstrating your respect for them and showing them how people should be treated.

Mindful communication is goal-driven and direct. Before you start a conversation with your child, consider what you'd like it to accomplish. The goal should not be to win an argument but to come up with a mutually beneficial solution to the problem at hand. For example, if you want your child to start doing homework earlier, say *why* it matters. If it's because you want them to have time to relax later, explain this. It may turn out that your child prefers to relax in the afternoon and you have more common ground than you thought.

Using clear and concise statements goes a long way. Though you want to be open to your child's input, there are some things that just need to get done. It's helpful to use plain language and adequate detail when giving directives: "Please put the clothes on your bed away before dinner at six o'clock." The task, expectation, and deadline are clear.

The skills described above can be challenging in practice. I recommend putting the greatest focus on your listening skills. When your child acts out, they're attempting to communicate something to you. The better you get at interpreting those attempts, the faster you can transition out of conflict and into problem-solving.

EXERCISE: Three POVs

Mindful communication requires the ability to see another person's point of view (POV). This exercise will teach you how to see one situation from three different viewpoints.

Consider a recent argument you had with your child. Recall, with as much detail as possible, the points of conflict and the arguments for each side.

1. At the top of a page in your notebook, write the subject of the argument (e.g., "homework").
2. Make three columns: "My POV," "Child's POV," and "Neutral POV."
3. In the "My POV" column, write why the issue was important to you: "I wanted him to finish his homework before dinner, so he could relax afterward." Next, write your initial goal for the conversation and the outcome: "I wanted a peaceful evening, but instead we got into a huge fight, ruining the afternoon." Is there anything you could have done differently? If so, write it down.

4. In the "Child's POV" column, make your best guess at why this was important to your child. Give them the benefit of the doubt and assume their goal was not to drive you crazy or argue for the sake of arguing. Perhaps they wanted a break after a long day at school. Now, write down their possible goal and the outcome: "He wanted a break to relax after school, but instead we got into a huge fight."

5. Under the "Neutral POV" column, write what you imagine a neutral observer would guess your goal and your child's goal were for the conversation.

6. Now, look at all three columns and reflect on how they differ, even though they're about a single situation. Below the columns, write down what it was like to see the situation from the other perspectives and what you can learn from it.

Begin practicing this skill mentally and in real time. It will take some work, but with repetition, you'll be on the way to communicating more effectively with your child.

The Art of Listening

Learning to listen well is an art that must be refined through intentional practice and discipline. It's also a huge component of communication. In order to become adept at mindful communication, you must hone your active and reflective listening skills.

Active listening is a multifaceted process. It includes maintaining eye contact and remaining attentive and open-minded, without interrupting, judging, or proposing solutions uninvited. You may be thinking, *That's a lot to do at once*. You're correct! But you're likely already doing many of these things when engaging with your child.

The next time you're talking to your child, focus on making consistent eye contact—not in a threatening way but in a way that demonstrates they have your full attention. Refrain from being on your phone or multitasking, so your kid sees that what they're saying is important to you. As you listen, focus not on how you want to reply but on what your child is saying. Notice if they're communicating anything about how they feel, since kids with ODD often act out in an attempt to manage strong emotions. If you notice yourself starting to judge, remind yourself to listen with the intent of understanding. Allow for silence. If your child does ask for your feedback, take a pause before you respond. Express your empathy for their situation, even if it's something minor like that they're grumpy because they didn't eat lunch. This shows that you're understanding how your child feels.

Reflective listening is taking in what the other person has said and repeating it back to them to ensure you've heard them correctly. It demonstrates you're seeking to understand your child's perspective. If you're having a conversation with your son about his frustrating experience at football practice, you can either repeat back verbatim what he last said ("you're really mad at Coach Reilly for benching you") or paraphrase ("it sounds like you're mad about being benched"). Paraphrasing can be trickier because you're more likely to include your own bias, so choose your words carefully. Asking for clarification is another element of reflective listening ("you're mad about Coach Reilly benching you, is that right?"). Though this may sound like a lot of work right now, with practice, these communication skills will come more readily.

Hearing What We Want to Hear

The writer William Whyte once astutely noted, "The great enemy of communication . . . is the illusion of it. We have talked enough; but we have not listened." This is what happens when we listen not to understand but rather to plan our next point or otherwise meet our own goals. It impedes our ability to problem-solve, connect, and empathize. I once worked with a young parent who really struggled to listen to what her son and I had worked on in session.

Whenever I'd begin summing up our sessions, she'd immediately say, "I know you must think I don't spend enough time with my child." Rather than listen to ways she could maximize the time she did spend with her son, she was too focused on defending herself to effectively strategize.

How often do you have a conversation with your child and find that you hear exactly what you knew you'd hear? Assuming you're not psychic, this is likely because you'd already decided what the outcome of the interaction would be—not because you're a bad parent but because you're used to conversations playing out a certain way. If you broach a discussion with your daughter about limiting her time on social media, and you already think you know how she'll respond, you'll probably unintentionally ignore anything she says that doesn't match your expectation. While this may seem like a small issue to you, it may be really important to her. Hearing what you want to hear instead of what is expressed limits your ability to connect.

Hearing What Is Said

Now, this is the good stuff! Hearing what is said is an essential element of mindful and effective communication. Clients often say that what they appreciate most about therapy is the chance to have someone really listen. There is tremendous healing in feeling heard and understood.

I once worked with a family of four on learning to hear what was actually said, not what they thought they'd heard. They'd gotten into the habit of making assumptions, and so we practiced over and over how to truly listen. I would have them get into pairs, have one person make a statement, and have the other repeat back what they heard the first person say. This may seem like a simple task, but you'd be surprised how hard it can be when you're not used to actually listening. After a month, each family member reported that their listening skills had improved, and they were arguing less. It's amazing what changes can be made when we sharpen our listening skills.

I know you're likely overwhelmed right now. You may feel unheard or misunderstood by your child. What if I told you that it would directly benefit *you* to listen to your child in such a way that you can truly understand, empathize, and hear them? By becoming a better communicator, you'll teach your child these same skills and reduce conflict. I know you want peace in your home and for your child to thrive. Investing time and effort into mindful communication skills will help you achieve these goals.

Conversation as Collaboration

Collaborative conversation is an important component of mindful communication. Like all other aspects of mindful communication, collaborative conversations are conducted with high levels of intention and openness. In their book *Unstoppable Learning*, educators Doug Fisher and Nancy Frey define these as conversations in which participants can "disagree without being disagreeable." Practically, this may look like listening to others without trying to change their minds, or talking openly about how you see the situation differently and agreeing to disagree.

People who are collaborating build on one another's ideas. Though as the parent you are the authority figure, collaborative conversation asks you to respect your child's input. That's not to say they have equal weight in decision-making but rather that you learn to value what they have to say and consider how you might take their desires into account before you make the final decision. This process is solution-focused, not problem-focused. The main goal is to find an agreeable resolution, not to dwell on points of contention.

Active and Reflective Listening

This exercise will help you grow your active and reflective listening skills and thereby improve how you communicate with your child. It may be a bit challenging, but it'll get easier with repetition. I recommend practicing these skills daily, with different people and in different circumstances. You can let your conversation partner in on what you're doing.

Begin a conversation with someone you know well, like a friend, spouse, or child. Start with an open-ended question, one they can't just answer with yes or no. ("What's been the best part of your day so far?")

As they respond, focus your attention on hearing every word. This includes eye contact, nodding, and other nonverbal behaviors indicating they have your undivided attention. Mentally repeat to yourself what you heard, and then, without any judgment, reflect it back to them. ("It sounds like you really enjoyed having lunch with Matt today.")

Let them reply, still giving them your undivided attention, then ask a clarifying question to show you want to understand their experience. ("Did you say you had a tuna sandwich on wheat?") Finally, are there any chances for you to demonstrate empathy? ("I'm glad you enjoyed your lunch outing!")

EXERCISE: What Do You Want from This Conversation?

Collaborative conversation is intentional and goal-directed. Too often, conversations with defiant children end up circling around familiar points of conflict with no resolution in sight. Though you can't control what your child brings up, having a clear idea of what you want to accomplish in the discussion can guide you toward solutions and keep the conversation on track. Let's work on an exercise to help you build your skills in this area.

Think about a conversation you need to have with your child in which you two are not on the same page. Choose something that's not too heavy but still important. Consider your stance on the subject. For example, maybe you want to talk to your son about spending too much time in his room with the door closed. Why does it concern you? Perhaps you worry he's becoming isolated, or it makes you uncomfortable that you don't know what he's up to. Whatever it is, consider without judgment why you hold your position. Write down your reasons in your notebook.

Now that you have a better understanding of your position, what do you want the outcome of your upcoming conversation to be? Sticking with the bedroom example, do you want him to spend more time with the family, or are you concerned that he's isolating himself because he's depressed? Your goal might become either inviting him to spend more time with family or checking in with him about his mood. "I'd love to spend more quality time with you," and, "I'm worried you might be feeling down," sound a lot different from—and a lot more loving than—"You're not allowed to close your bedroom door." Both of these examples express your concerns rather than demands.

Write down your goals for the discussion before you sit down with your child. It may be helpful to share those goals with your child, because it shows you're making an effort to relate to them in a different way. When you're ready, initiate the conversation, and if you find yourself getting lost in the weeds, steer yourself back to your goals.

Setting Boundaries

In general, families struggling with ODD are not known for having good boundaries when communicating. Loud arguments, aggressive speech, and threats are probably common occurrences in your home. These boundary violations often derail productive communication and problem-solving. Setting appropriate boundaries can be challenging, and it takes time to get everyone on the same page, but it's a crucial part of mindful communication.

To set useful conversational boundaries, first identify where they're needed. For example, do arguments get disrespectful? If so, then *respect* is a boundary that needs to be established. How can you set that boundary? Maybe you commit to not raising your voice when your child raises theirs, or stick to constructive statements instead of insults. Rather than, "Your room looks like a pigsty," you could try, "Please straighten out your room." (Remember, I said this would be hard!)

Refraining from threats is another boundary many parents have to create. It's common for both parents and kids to struggle with this one, but threats do little to resolve conflict; in fact, they practically guarantee it will escalate. See how your conversations change when you're no longer constantly threatening your child with grounding or the loss of a favorite device. You'll probably soon find that conversations are more diplomatic and less contentious.

Helping Your Child Set Boundaries

Children with ODD need clear and consistent boundaries. Though they may initially resist them, they benefit greatly from the structure and stability they provide. Their internal sense of chaos can be frightening to them, and boundaries help give them order in ways they can't yet do on their own. Helping your child set boundaries in how they communicate is essential to managing their ODD. The goal is to help kids identify expectations for how they're treated and how they treat others.

It can be helpful to start with the most frequently occurring disruptive behavior in your home. Many times, *yelling* is the target behavior. When your child is in a calm state, talk to them about how yelling affects you and ask them how your yelling impacts them. Establish your house as a "yell-free" zone. Next, come up with a phrase you can say to each other when one of you begins to yell. ("It's okay to be mad, but it's not okay to yell.") This acknowledges the other person's emotions while setting limits on behavior you've agreed is unacceptable. Model using these skills the next time your child yells at you, and if you catch yourself yelling at them, recognize you violated their boundaries and apologize. When you notice your child setting and maintaining healthy boundaries, praise them. This is a major step in strengthening mindful communication.

Nonviolent Communication

Another means of communicating more mindfully with your child is through nonviolent communication. This skill set aims to increase compassion, connection, and accountability. The goal is to help each party in the conversation get their needs met in adaptive, respectful ways.

Defiant and oppositional behavior is marked by *violent communication*, by which I mean yelling, name-calling, judging, blaming, and defensiveness (not physical violence, though that can also occur). Violent communication makes it hard to effectively problem-solve or build connection with your child. Have you noticed that when you and your child argue, you feel emotionally distant from them? That's because the violent nature of the communication has made it feel unsafe to be connected—for both you *and* your child.

I once worked with a young client, Daniel, who had huge meltdowns when his parents told him no. As a result, each time his father, Arturo, anticipated turning down one of Daniel's requests, he'd shut

Loving-Kindness Meditation

This meditation is intended to help increase positive feelings, warmth, and compassion toward your child. Set a timer for 10 minutes. Get comfortable, close your eyes, and spend two minutes focusing on your breath, inhaling deeply through your nose, then slowly exhaling through your mouth.

Relax your body from head to feet, one area at a time: face, neck, shoulders, and so on down your body.

With your eyes closed, think of someone in your life who loves you and makes you feel happy, like a family member, friend, or mentor. This person doesn't have to still be living or part of your life. Imagine they're standing to your right and radiating their love to you, sending you well wishes, joy, and protection. Feel their kindness and compassion.

Now imagine you're encircled by people who love you deeply and fully. Envision your family, children, friends, and mentors surrounding you with their hopes for your good health, well-being, and peace. Take in the warmth and love you feel around you.

Focus on the person standing to your right. Send the love you're basking in back to them. They, like you, want to be happy, at peace. Direct your warmth, kindness, and love to this person. In your mind, repeat these words three times: *May you be safe, may you be joyful, may you be free of suffering.*

Now imagine another person you love, perhaps your child. This person also hopes to have a joyful life, just as you do. Send them warm wishes. Repeat these words in your mind three times: *May your life be filled with wellness, health, and joy.*

Next, think of an acquaintance you don't know well and feel neutral toward. You and this person both wish to have a nice life. Send them your wishes for wellness, repeating these words three times in your mind: *Just as I hope to, may you also live with joy and be free of suffering.*

Finally, think of the whole wide world. See the earth in its wholeness in front of you. Send warmth and love to all living beings in the world, who also want to be happy, just as you do. Repeat these words in your mind three times: *Just as I hope to, may you live with joy, health, and safety.*

Take several more deep breaths. Slowly exhale. When you're ready, open your eyes. How are you feeling? Do this exercise whenever you want to connect to your feelings of loving-kindness for your child.

down emotionally. Arturo did this as a way of protecting himself from the powerful negative emotions he felt in response to his son's behavior, but it was creating a long-term problem for him: It became impossible for him to feel compassion for Daniel's disappointment. Daniel interpreted the shutdown as a sign his dad didn't care about his feelings, which further fueled his tantrums. Though his dad cared very much, the communication patterns the two had established actually perpetuated the cycle of violent and aggressive communication. After lots of practice, Arturo worked to stay emotionally open during tough conversations with Daniel. He soon learned that the more he let his guard down, the more empathy he could show his son. In just a few weeks, the frequency and intensity of the tantrums were reduced.

First, Do No Harm

As parents, our greatest goal is to protect our children from harm. We go to great lengths to keep them physically safe with helmets, seat belts, and check-in texts when they're out with friends. But we sometimes overlook their *emotional* safety, in part because, as a society, we're not taught to value emotional well-being the same way we value physical well-being. So how do we learn to protect our kids' emotional safety? By learning to be gentle and empathetic when we communicate with them.

Overhauling how you relate to your child probably sounds like a daunting task, but it's possible—and necessary! In this chapter, you've learned communication strategies aimed at decreasing negative habits. In many ways, they all boil down to the maxim "do no harm." The purpose of these skills is to equip you to manage your child's behavioral problem without getting caught up in their chaos. Regulating your own intense emotions through mindfulness and self-care will help you maintain composure when faced with emotional eruptions. The better you can handle your big emotions, the more likely you'll be to demonstrate empathy toward your child when they're having difficulty regulating theirs. In doing so, you'll show them that you understand and care about their feelings.

Doing this well requires you to make some changes. Yelling, screaming, name-calling, insulting, sarcasm, blaming, and judging all have to go. Even if your child starts in on these behaviors, you can't reciprocate. This will be hard, but it's imperative. Remember the saying, "If your friend jumped off a bridge, would you?" The same goes for how you communicate with your kiddo. Just because they scream doesn't mean you have to do the same. Instead, you get to model a new way of responding.

Choosing Words with Care

In everyday life, you might not think much about the words you choose when talking to your loved ones. You likely speak more casually with your child or spouse than with your boss. This is generally normal and appropriate, but when we fall into unhealthy communication habits, it becomes imperative to understand the meaning and power of our words.

Remember that mindful communication is *intentional*. Purposefully choosing the words we use with our children is an opportunity for growth. Consider the two phrases, "Can you just be quiet?" and, "Can you please lower your voice?" Both phrases are requesting the other person quiet down, but which one sounds more respectful? Though they have the same meaning, the first statement sounds more like a demand while the second feels like more of a request. Let's try another one: "I'm sick of you disrespecting me!" versus, "I'm frustrated because I feel disrespected." By simply changing a few words, I went from placing blame to expressing my feelings.

By being selective with your language, you can build connection instead of create distance. It also allows your child to better understand limits. For example, parents will often say things like, "Can you clean your room?" Of course, the child *can* clean their room—whether or not they *will* is a different story. Directing the child to, "Please clean your room before we leave at noon," is a lot more specific. It allows less room for confusion or wiggling out of responsibility. As with all aspects of mindful communication, learning to be intentional with your words will help you form more positive communication habits with your child.

Action Plan: A Respectful Conversation

It's time to put your mindful communication skills into practice! Your assignment is to initiate a respectful conversation with your child.

Before you get started . . .

- Decide what to talk about—a television show you're watching, how their day has gone, etc.
- Choose two skills described in this chapter (such as active listening, nonviolent communication, or collaboration) to use during the conversation. Make one a listening skill.
- Select a time and place where you know your child will be most open to talking, perhaps on the way home from school or during dinner.

Once you're ready to have the conversation . . .

- Initiate the conversation by inviting them to share their thoughts on the topic you chose.
- During the discussion, practice the two skills you selected.
- Notice how your child responds when you use the skills. For example, if you chose active listening, how does your child react when you reflect what they've said?
- Did you notice anything different about the experience after using your skills?

I know that the best-laid plans can get derailed by a bad mood or other realities of daily life. Just remember, if this conversation doesn't go as planned, you'll always have another opportunity. I suggest practicing this exercise several times per week. Jotting down in your notebook what skills were most effective will help you track your progress.

Takeaways

- Mindful communication is respectful, intentional, and nonviolent.
- Mindful communication can help you manage conflict with your child in healthy ways.
- Active and reflective listening skills are tools to help you become a more effective parent.
- Changing your communication habits is hard work but worth the effort.
- Collaborating with your child when there's a problem creates solutions and teaches problem-solving skills.
- Learning nonviolent communication skills can help you get unstuck.
- Learning to choose your words carefully can make communication go more smoothly.
- Changing habits is hard, but not changing can be even harder.

PART TWO

Taking Care of Your Child

CHAPTER FIVE

Oppositional Defiant Disorder: Mapping the Trouble Spots

"Why Do They Act Like That?": ODD and Skills Deficits

Do you ever catch yourself asking why your child acts the way they do? Or worse, have other people asked you that question? If so, you're not alone. Children with ODD often behave in ways that are angry, unpredictable, and out of control. In order to understand what causes these difficult behaviors, it's important to know what behaviors lead to an ODD diagnosis.

According to the fifth edition of the American Psychiatric Association's *Diagnostic and Statistical Manual of Mental Disorders* (*DSM-5*), which defines criteria for mental health conditions, ODD is characterized by a "pattern of angry/irritable mood, argumentative/defiant behavior, or vindictiveness." Let's look at how those characteristics show up in real life.

Angry/irritable mood: Children with ODD are often grumpy or downright angry. Their moods can shift in an instant, sometimes for no apparent reason. They get annoyed easily and may hold on to resentment longer than expected.

Argumentative/defiant behavior: These children may argue with peers, siblings, parents, and teachers, with little or no provocation. They don't seem to understand the concept of authority figures and behave as though rules are optional. They may purposefully annoy others. When they're caught misbehaving or making a mistake, even a minor one, they deny responsibility.

Vindictiveness: Vindictive, spiteful behavior is common with these kids. You may find them plotting revenge that can range from innocuous to downright dangerous. They may wish ill on others.

It's important to note that the behaviors associated with ODD are frequent and persistent. They're not the result of developmental phases or a child having a bad week, but rather a pattern of behavior that lasts for at least six months and greatly impacts the child and/or those around them. These behaviors may show up at home, in school, when socializing, or all of the above.

Angry, irritable, argumentative, defiant, vindictive—these are not adjectives that inspire feelings of empathy. Empathy, however, is exactly what ODD kids need. Think about times when you've felt argumentative or defiant. You no doubt felt, in the moment, that you had good reasons for acting that way. In the same way, these children aren't behaving defiantly because it's enjoyable or helps solve their problems. They're acting out because they don't feel they have a choice—they lack the skills to manage their feelings and resolve conflicts in more adaptive ways. They're struggling.

Children with ODD don't yet have the psychological skills to behave differently, so a big part of your job is to help identify which skills your child needs to develop to help them meet their goals.

Understanding Skills Deficits

The term *skills deficit* refers to the emotional, social, and cognitive (thinking) abilities that are undeveloped or underdeveloped in your child. This is about development, not intelligence.

It's easy to take for granted the skills necessary to complete seemingly simple tasks such as ordering a meal at a restaurant. You must be able to determine your hunger level, read the menu, select an entrée, and so on. In the same way, it's easy to underestimate the skill set your child needs to navigate through an average day. Children with ODD are commonly lacking or lagging in skill sets like emotion regulation, executive functioning, and social skills. Let's look at each of these areas.

Emotion regulation is the ability to understand and manage our emotions—even strong ones—in healthy, effective ways. A related concept is *distress tolerance*, the ability to ride out painful, overwhelming emotions. Kids with ODD struggle to regulate their intense feelings. They often cannot properly identify or express their internal experiences (feelings, sensations, thoughts) and thus can't state their needs clearly, especially when under stress. Screaming, crying, tantrums, defiance, and physical aggression in response to stressors all suggest deficits in emotion regulation. When your child has difficulty identifying and managing an intense emotional state, they use these behaviors (unsuccessfully) to "get rid of" it. Until the child learns other ways of responding, the behaviors will persist.

Executive functioning is a clinical term for advanced cognitive processes like paying attention, planning, self-control, problem-solving, anticipating consequences, and mentally shifting from one activity to another. When ODD kids become overwhelmed by their feelings, it impacts those thought processes, because stressed-out brains don't think very clearly. The prefrontal cortex (the region of the brain most responsible for executive functioning) is not completely developed until around age 25, and conditions such as ADHD can directly impact executive functioning, making these complex skills even harder to acquire. Your child's skills deficits in this area might show up as rigid thinking, impulsive behavior, not considering the consequences of their actions, and struggling to shift from one task to another (e.g., from playing at recess to starting an English lesson).

Finally, *social skills* refers to our interpersonal effectiveness—our ability to engage with others, read social cues, follow social norms, and understand how our actions impact others. Social skills are essential to making and keeping friends, succeeding at work, establishing romantic relationships, and generally functioning in society. Children with ODD often struggle in interpersonal relationships because they don't have the emotional literacy of their peers. Social interactions leave them feeling confused, ineffective, and criticized, because they don't understand why people are responding negatively to them.

Deficits or developmental delays in emotion regulation, executive functioning, and social skills may sound scary, but take heart: There are tools that you and your child can learn to bridge those developmental gaps.

They're Doing the Best They Can

In his book *The Explosive Child*, Dr. Ross Greene writes, "Kids do well if they can." That's true of your child as well, even in their most difficult moments. They're acting out because they don't know a better way of getting their needs met.

Imagine how annoying it would be to try to do something that was naturally very difficult for you, only to fail over and over again—and sometimes get punished for your efforts! This is your child's experience every day. That's why it's imperative to remind yourself that your child is sincerely trying. Etch these words into your mind: *My child is doing the best they can.*

Once children have the tools to manage challenging situations, they no longer feel the need for explosive behavior. So let's turn to the strategies you can use to help them gain those tools. We'll start by examining some of the typical "trouble spots" where you and your child are likely struggling and take a closer look at the specific skills your child needs in order to make real gains.

Trouble Spot: Inflexibility

Inflexibility most often shows up in situations when things don't go according to our expectations or desires and we struggle to adapt to the unexpected circumstances. Kids with ODD are chronically inflexible. They have great difficulty "going with the flow" and managing the demands of change, disappointment, differing schedules, and uncertain expectations. Any deviations can lead to immediate, intense meltdowns.

Children learn and develop at different rates. When talking with other parents, you may have noticed that some kids sleep better or eat a wider array of foods. The same goes for flexibility. Though most of us take it for granted, flexibility actually requires a lot of cognitive and emotional resources. Though inflexible behaviors are challenging, there are many strategies to address them, if you know what skills your child is lacking.

What Do They Need to Learn?

To reduce inflexibility, the most important thing children with ODD must learn is how to identify and label their own emotions and thoughts so they can understand how situations impact those emotions and thoughts. Learning to recognize their personal triggers is essential, but understanding their emotions comes first. As your child learns to recognize their feelings, they can begin to calm themselves before the emotional intensity becomes too strong to manage.

Tolerating distress is also vital. Since effectively managing uncomfortable feelings is a necessary skill set, children with ODD need to strengthen their ability to sit with discomfort and to express anger, frustration, and sadness appropriately.

All kids—and adults, for that matter—can have difficulty shifting from one type of task to another, especially when the new task is very different from the first. Children with ODD benefit greatly from learning to manage the mental demands of, for example, moving from playing a video game to doing homework. Closely related is learning to plan ahead, which involves thinking systemically about how future events might unfold.

Another common skills deficit is difficulty inhibiting impulsive behaviors, which essentially means ODD kids need to learn *self-control*. Teaching them how to pause before acting and thereby manage their behavior allows them to have greater flexibility in challenging situations. They can also get better at inhibiting the impulse to follow the first idea that crosses their mind by learning the step-by-step problem-solving process of identifying the problem, exploring possible solutions, deciding which would be most helpful, and then trying out the solution.

Alternatives to Conflict

The purpose of this section, here and in the chapters that follow, is to provide practical tools to address each trouble spot and help reduce conflict with your child. These skills can also help your child with emotion regulation and executive functioning. It's important to practice all skills in the Alternatives to Conflict section when your child is in a calm state. Trying to teach new skills when they're behaviorally escalated will be ineffective.

Inflexibility in children is often related to unregulated emotions. If a child doesn't have the vocabulary to describe what they're experiencing, they're more likely to erupt. To help them appropriately express their experience, teach them to verbally label their feelings, thoughts, and bodily sensations (e.g., "I feel worried," or, "When I get mad, my body feels hot"). Rating the intensity level of the feeling on a five-point scale (five being the most intense) also helps, because they can learn to seek help when the feelings are still at a manageable one or two.

Helping your child learn to express their needs in healthy ways can also reduce conflict. You can encourage this by wondering out loud what your child may need from you or another. For example, if your child is pestering your partner while they're trying to work, you can say, "I wonder if you need some attention right now and aren't sure how to ask for it. Can I help you with that?"

Another skill to help reduce conflict is to expressly state how their behavior impacts you: "When you high-fived me after the big game yesterday, I felt really happy," or, "It hurt my feelings when you said you hated me." Children with ODD are often so wrapped up in their own internal experience that they cannot in the moment understand that others have feelings, too.

Since uncomfortable feelings are part of life, one of the main goals of working with ODD children is to increase their self-control and ability to tolerate distress. Learning to pause before acting can drastically reduce the frequency and intensity of their outbursts. When you notice your child is getting upset, encourage them to take space to

Collaborative Conversation

The purpose of a collaborative conversation is to come up with a mutually beneficial solution to a problem. Collaborating helps model problem-solving, negotiation skills, and respectful dialogue. It also teaches children that their voices matter. Often, children just need to express how they feel, even if they don't get their way. Below is an example of a collaborative conversation between twelve-year-old Jack and his dad.

Jack: I'm sick of you turning off the Wi-Fi at 9:00! It's not fair! I'm not a little kid. You can't control me!

Dad: I know you're not a little kid. I get that you think this is unfair and feel angry about it. I also know it feels terrible to feel controlled.

Jack: Then why do you keep doing it?

Dad: I understand you feel mad, and I'm open to other ideas. What time do you think would be reasonable to turn off the Wi-Fi that would still give you plenty of sleep?

Jack: Midnight.

Dad: You have to get up for practice at six. Will that give you enough sleep?

Jack: I don't care about sleep!

Dad: Hmm. How do you play when you haven't slept well?

Jack: Like crap.

Dad: Okay, maybe 12:00 is too late during the week. How about 12:00 on weekends, and earlier during the week?

Jack: That doesn't suck that bad, I guess.

Dad: Let's try that, then.

calm down by deep breathing for two minutes, squeezing a stress ball, or thinking of a relaxing scene or image. Intense exercise can also be helpful, because it helps release the tension associated with inflexibility. These skills will take time to learn, so be patient.

Additionally, when possible, prepare your child ahead of time for routine changes—for instance, "We're going to the mall after school today, so you'll have your snack in the car," or, "You get thirty minutes of phone time before homework. I'll remind you when you have five minutes left." This can help reduce emotional overload when it comes to schedule changes or shifting from one task to another.

These alternatives to conflict are your first set of tools to help increase peace in your home and equip your child with the skill sets needed to thrive. The skills laid out in these sections are meant to build on and complement one another. I'd recommend trying one or two every few days rather than trying them all at once. The goal is to find the ones that work best for your child and keep using them.

Trouble Spot: Defiance of Authority

Defiance of authority figures is a hallmark of ODD. It's an *externalizing behavior*—it's directed outward, at other people and the environment. An escalation of defiance is usually what brings parents to my office. Tantrums are one thing; flipping off a teacher is another entirely.

Defiance of authority figures comes in different forms. It can be as minor as disregarding advice or as extreme as assaulting a parent. Many mistakenly believe that children with ODD are naturally disrespectful or argumentative, but that's not usually the case. Typically, defiance is a symptom of reinforced patterns (behaviors that have been repeated so often they've become habits), difficulty regulating emotions, and poor impulse control. Like so many other problematic ODD behaviors, it's simply an ineffective way of coping with stress and discomfort.

In many ways, defiance is a natural part of the human condition. Think about a two-year-old who screams at her dad when told she can't have a cookie. She doesn't understand that her dad is holding out because it's almost dinnertime. She interprets him only as an obstacle to the thing she wants most in the moment. It will take time, guidance, and consistency for her to learn to follow adult directives, even if that means enduring disappointment or frustration. Children struggling with ODD need to learn the same thing, but the nature of their challenges means they're often learning it later in life than most.

What Do They Need to Learn?

In basic terms, children who defy authority need to learn to manage difficult emotions like frustration and disappointment in more effective ways. They struggle to find the language to express their feelings appropriately and are often flooded with unpleasant emotions and negative feedback from the people on the receiving end of their tantrums. They also likely struggle with feeling safe enough to share their feelings. Instead, they lash out by talking back or doing the opposite of what they're told.

I once worked with an eleven-year-old boy who would have blow-ups every morning before school. It drove his parents crazy, but the more they demanded he hurry up and get ready, the more resistant he became. Eventually, he shared that he hated getting ready in the morning because he knew he wouldn't see his parents until they got home from work in the evening. His defiance had to do with feeling sad about missing his parents, but until he felt safe enough to share his vulnerable feelings, his parents had no way to interpret his seemingly angry behavior.

Kids with ODD also need help understanding why it's not okay to be disrespectful to adults. In our society, children are expected to obey adults, especially those in positions of authority (parents, babysitters, teachers, etc.). This is what we call a *social norm*. Though the child may never agree with the hierarchy of authority, it's essential that they learn to respond to it appropriately, because their ability to do so will have a huge impact on their current and future functioning. Defiant adults have trouble holding jobs, maintaining relationships, and staying out of trouble generally.

Lack of self-control also plays a huge role in defiance. It indicates struggles with key executive-functioning skills, particularly impulse inhibition, or the ability *not* to do something we feel like doing. Kids with ODD struggle greatly to manage their impulses and anticipate the consequences of their actions, which is related to the key executive function of *planning*. For example, nine-year-old Malea is angry that her teacher won't let her be the first to go out to recess. She has the urge to get out of her seat and go anyway, so she does. Malea didn't consider *not* leaving her seat as an option—or the consequences she'd experience for disobeying her teacher.

Alternatives to Conflict

When kids become defiant, it's usually because they're angry, but as you know from chapter 3, there are often other feelings beneath the anger. Talking about hard feelings normalizes them for your child—everyone has them. Teaching that all feelings are okay, even the uncomfortable ones, allows your child to feel less stigmatized for their negative emotions. Empathy also goes a long way in reducing conflict. Think back to times you experienced frustration as a child or adolescent, and let your child know you understand their feelings without trying to change or judge them. *Your* capacity to tolerate their negative emotions will help increase *their* capacity as well.

Work to help your child understand that their feelings and thoughts impact their behavior. Though all feelings are okay, not all actions are, and while we can't control every situation, we can learn to control our behavior. When you're in a situation where your child typically becomes triggered, remind them that their emotions don't have to be in charge and that they have more power than they think to influence what happens by making good behavioral choices.

Remember to Take Care of You

Right now, you're in the thick of this process. As you help your child grow and learn new skills, it's important to keep taking care of yourself. I find that parents often have trouble remembering that their own self-care is a big part of their child's treatment. Of the self-care tools you've built into your routine, which work best? You don't need a lot of different self-care activities; a few effective ones will do.

Here are a few ways to nourish your own needs:

- *Go for a walk, run, or bike ride.*
- *Call a good friend.*
- *Go on a date with your spouse/partner.*
- *Get a good night's rest.*
- *Eat a healthy meal.*
- *Do something you love to do, even if it's as simple as looking at baby animal pictures on Pinterest.*
- *Tell yourself all the things that went right in the last 48 hours, even if it's just, "They got my order right at Starbucks."*
- *Express your creativity: write, draw, color, build something.*
- *Listen to your favorite song.*

Defiance of authority is usually more an impulse-control issue than an intentional attempt at manipulation. Counting can be a great tool to help your child reduce their impulsivity. For young kids, try having them slowly count to ten before acting. For older children, have them count backward from 100 by sevens. These tasks take concentration—just what your child needs to distract them from their intense feelings. If counting is too challenging initially, have them make a fist with both hands and hold for five seconds; they can do this three times in a row before choosing how to proceed.

Try out these new tools over the next few weeks. As with all skills discussed in the Alternative to Conflict sections, limit yourself to one new skill at a time so as not to overwhelm yourself or your child. And practice skills when your child is in a calm state; trying to teach new skills when they're behaviorally escalated will be ineffective and frustrating for you both.

Trouble Spot: Emotional Volatility

Children with ODD struggle with emotional volatility far beyond the basic moodiness that we all experience at times, transforming from happy and upbeat one minute to enraged the next. While children are typically excitable, playful, and carefree, ODD kids can be chronically grumpy and pessimistic and often seem unusually burdened for their age. That's because emotional volatility is a stressful state to be in.

Another term for this is *emotional dysregulation*. When a child with ODD experiences intense feelings, they can't effectively regulate their emotions by bringing themselves up from a low or down from a high, back to the calm state where people generally function best. They can be quite literally out of control during a meltdown, unable to modulate emotions. Think of a time when you were unusually upset and overcome by emotions. Recall how it felt in your body when the negative thoughts, feelings, or images were racing through you, out of your control. Now consider what it would be like to experience that daily, maybe several times per day. Your child's emotional dysregulation is likely both exhausting and terrifying for them, so it's important to learn how to express empathy, even when they're behaving in ways that are difficult for you.

Your child's unpredictable emotions can make daily life challenging. Many parents feel like they're walking on eggshells from the moment they wake up to the time their child goes to sleep. The roller coaster of emotions impacts everyone in the household, including siblings. It may feel like a lose-lose situation for everyone involved.

What Do They Need to Learn?

When it comes to emotional volatility, kids need to learn two essential skills: how to regulate their emotions and how to self-soothe.

Emotion-regulation skills have and will come up often throughout this book, because the ability to successfully manage intense emotions is a foundational goal in treating ODD. But what does that look like in action? What are people doing when they regulate themselves this way? In order to regulate your emotions, you need to be aware of the impact your feelings have on your thoughts and behaviors. That's why helping your child gain a strong vocabulary and understanding of their feelings is essential. Once they have words (*happy, angry, sad*) for their experience, they're no longer stuck with intense, nameless, scary sensations. Identifying feelings is the first step in the emotion-regulation process.

Self-soothing, meanwhile, is the ability to calm yourself when you're upset, and it's a fundamental part of childhood development. We learn to self-soothe from our primary caregivers. Think of how you cared for your child when they cried as a baby, feeding them, rocking them, or changing their diaper. Through these daily acts of care, you helped teach them to soothe themselves. Childhood is a period to refine these skills, but not all children do that equally well; some require additional support to learn to effectively calm themselves when upset.

Children with ODD have significant difficulty self-soothing when they're emotionally escalated. Because of this, they're often very sensitive; their prickly nature acts as armor. Self-soothing is especially difficult for those with high levels of sensitivity, skills deficits, and/or delays in executive functioning. You'll need to act as a scaffold until they gain the skills to manage by themselves.

Alternatives to Conflict

Below are some more skills aimed at increasing emotional stability in your child. They can be used alone or with skills from the previous Alternatives to Conflict sections. Remember, new skills should not be taught when your child is having an outburst. Our brains learn best when we're calm.

To reduce emotional volatility, your child must be able to identify, label, and rate the intensity of their emotions. Continue to work with your child on these skills—they can't overlearn them!

Learning ways to ask for help when overwhelmed can increase your child's ability to stabilize their mood. Sometimes just telling someone that you feel overwhelmed reduces the intensity of the feelings. You and your child (and siblings, teachers, and so on) could use a code word like *freeze* or *pause* to signal that they seem overloaded. Coaching kids to "freeze" when their feelings are at a three out of five can reduce outbursts. When they freeze, ask them to look around and identify three different colors and three distinct sounds and touch three items. From there, they can think about their next steps and proceed accordingly.

Creating "calm-down cards" can be a fun way to practice emotion-regulation skills. Using index cards they can keep in their backpack or wallet, work with your child to come up with three to five activities they can do when they feel upset, such as deep breathing, listening to their favorite song, doing jumping jacks, petting a dog, or taking a pause. I use these cards with kids from ages three to eighteen (and even with adults!) and have found them very helpful.

Many helpful meditation and relaxation apps are also available for free or little cost. I like the Breathe app because you can set reminders to practice deep breathing throughout the day. GoNoodle is great for younger children, and Insight Timer is a nice option for teens.

Another technique to help your child learn to reduce intense emotions is to have them pass an ice cube from hand to hand until it melts or place it on their wrists' pulse points. The cold temperature can gently shock their system into the present moment, so they're no longer stuck inside their internal experience. Try this when you notice your child is likely to be triggered, to decrease the chance of an outburst.

Finally, self-care is as important for your child as it is for you. Help them come up with ways they can tend to themselves daily, including art, journaling, games, exercise, and spending time with friends. I don't count TV, device time, or video games as self-care, because they let kids zone out, and the goal is to stay present in the moment.

You've been given many skills in these Alternatives to Conflict sections. That's not intended to overwhelm you but to provide you with lots of options to build your child's toolbox of coping skills. Don't be disheartened if some of them don't work—not every tool will be useful for every person—but I recommend trying one skill several times before discarding it. Give yourself and your child some grace. Learning new habits is hard!

Action Plan: Identify Three Problematic Behaviors

The following action plan will help you identify your child's most frequent problematic behaviors and under what conditions they typically present.

First, write some of your child's problematic behaviors in your notebook, being as specific as possible: "yelling at me when he wakes up late for school," "throwing a tantrum when we leave the park." Label each behavior with one of the categories discussed in chapter 5 (inflexibility, defiance of authority, and emotion regulation). Then rate each behavior on a scale of one to five, with one being the least extreme (not making the bed the first time they're asked) and five being the most (hitting adults).

Now choose a behavior from each of the categories, making sure it doesn't exceed a four. (Rome wasn't built in a day.) Get specific about these three behaviors. Write down the who, what, when, where, and why. For example:

Problematic behavior: Talking back when given directives
Category: Defiance of authority
Who: Parents, teachers, and coaches
What: Speaks disrespectfully to adults, doesn't follow directives
When: When given directives or told to do something they don't want to do
Where: Home, school, soccer field
Why: Usually tired or anxious

Now that you've identified the specific contexts of these behaviors, you can more effectively target them for change, as we'll discuss in chapters 6, 7, and 8.

Takeaways

- Children with ODD are not bad kids.
- Undeveloped or underdeveloped skills are often the cause of defiant behavior.
- These kids are doing the best they can.
- Flexibility (the ability to go with the flow, switch from one task to another, or manage feelings when things don't go as expected) can be especially challenging for kids with ODD.
- Defiance often occurs because the child has learned over time that it's an effective way of communicating.
- Emotional volatility, tantrums, and mood swings are ways of expressing overwhelming emotions.
- Don't forget to take care of yourself during this process!

CHAPTER SIX

Your ODD Toolbox

Introduction: Learning Your ABCs

The last chapter focused on the skills deficits associated with ODD and the roles inflexibility, defiance, and emotional volatility play in ODD symptoms. Now that you understand those trouble spots, let's look at three important tools to help improve your child's behavior. The concepts in this chapter will be used throughout the remainder of the book, because they're foundational skills needed to reduce acting-out behaviors. I'm going to call them the ABCs: alternatives, boundaries, and consequences.

Alternatives

Remember Dr. Ross Greene's assertion that kids do well if they can? Treating ODD relies on understanding that children act out not because they want to cause trouble but because they don't have the skills to handle things differently. This is where the first ABC concept comes into play: alternatives.

Alternative adaptive behaviors can take the place of your kid's current unhelpful ones. Think of alternatives as better options. For example, if your child begins yelling when you limit their TV time, the goal is to find a suitable alternative behavior to yelling.

Again, it's helpful to view your child's problematic behaviors as coping strategies, albeit ineffective ones. We shouldn't take away or punish their current coping strategies without giving them more adaptive new ones. Because children with ODD often have great difficulty breaking behavioral habits, your task is to help them see they have better options for managing their feelings and getting their needs met.

I once worked with the family of a nine-year-old named Emme, who always became very agitated before bedtime. Every night, her parents had to force her to complete her nighttime routine, which often took an entire hour. Upon closer investigation, it turned out Emme was afraid of the dark. Her nighttime routine made her anxious because she'd soon be alone in her dark bedroom. By teaching her deep breathing and a visualization exercise, her parents gave her a new skill set to manage her feelings more effectively. Going to bed became easier, and Emme felt more confident as a result of gaining new skills.

Boundaries

Boundaries are limits meant to build structure, safety, and consistency. They create expectations and rules for behavior, so I'll be using the terms *boundaries*, *rules*, and *expectations* more or less interchangeably. An example of a boundary is, "It's okay to spend time with friends but not to stay out all night," or, "It's fine to disagree on an issue, but it's not okay to yell." Appropriate boundaries let children feel safe and secure in their environment, which is why children with ODD may thrive at school while struggling at home.

Instituting boundaries can be challenging, because beyond basic manners, most families run on a fluid set of rules and assumptions that change over time. An ODD child's defiance of authority can challenge this loose structure.

The families I work with seem to struggle most with boundaries that are too rigid, too loose, or inconsistent. Each comes with its own set of problems.

Rigid boundaries allow no room for mistakes or negotiation and rarely take into account the child's input or needs. Examples include expecting a child to get straight A's or to wake up at 6:00 a.m. even on weekends.

Loose boundaries give the child more freedom than they're capable of handling—for example, not giving your teen a curfew or setting no standards for how they perform in school.

Inconsistent boundaries are rules and expectations that are not regularly enforced. This can cause anxiety and rebellion in children. A child who has had their Xbox taken away for not doing their homework may whine until their parents give it back, learning in the process that they can successfully bypass rules. Inconsistent boundaries are especially challenging for kids with ODD, who need appropriate, consistent, and firm boundaries so they know what to expect and what's expected of them.

Years ago, I worked with a single dad named Michael and his son, Drew. Michael had good intentions, but the boundaries he set were too rigid, prompting Drew to basically say, "Screw it!" There were so many rules that it was also hard for Michael, who worked two jobs, to enforce them with any regularity. He felt like a failure, and Drew felt controlled. Working with them to create less rigid, more realistic boundaries made all the difference. After several weeks, Michael felt more confident in his parenting because he was able to be consistent, and Drew was happier because his dad respected his boundaries and didn't flip-flop on rules as much.

Learning to institute appropriate boundaries helps create a sense of order in your home. Once you've set healthy limits and expectations, the work becomes guiding your child's actions toward respecting those boundaries.

Consequences

Consequences are an important means of helping your children understand the effects of their choices. Children with ODD often have a difficult time anticipating the results of their actions. Implementing consequences helps mold their behavior in adaptive ways.

For our purposes, *consequences* will refer to any results of a behavior, whether they're positive, neutral, or negative. I'll also distinguish between natural and logical consequences. *Natural consequences* happen on their own, without any intervention from adults. If your child forgets their lunch at home, the natural consequence is that they're hungry. *Logical consequences*, on the other hand, usually require adult intervention and are often more punitive. For example, if a child doesn't clean their room, a parent might restrict them from playing with friends. Generally, allowing a child to experience natural consequences works better, because it teaches the child cause and effect.

This book will help you plan how and when to implement consequences. But remember, this plan *must* also include positive consequences, which reinforce (reward) desirable behaviors. If you notice your child really focusing on their homework, for instance, you could praise their effort. Positive consequences are an even more powerful way to shape your child's behavior than negative ones—even though punishment is often the first thing parents reach for when stressed. Of course, there may be times when punishment is a necessary consequence, so we'll also explore appropriate and reasonable methods of instituting negative consequences.

Now that you've added the ABCs to your ODD toolbox, you're on your way to helping your child gain the skills they need to more effectively manage their ODD symptoms.

Consequences: The Power of the Positive

Now that we've covered the different types of consequences, we'll dive into how to use them with your child. The main consequence we'll use in this program is *positive reinforcement*—a tool to help shape a child's behavior by motivating them toward desirable changes. A way to positively reinforce good dining habits might be to offer an extra five minutes of snuggle time before bed if your child finishes their dinner. The child will be more likely to do so, because they want the additional time with you.

Parents often remark that positive reinforcement feels like rewarding their child for just doing what they're supposed to. But reinforcement is in action all the time for adults. Why do most people get up and go to work each morning? Because money is a powerful motivator! I'm not suggesting you pay your child for good behavior, but learning what motivates them is a critical step in helping them build better life skills.

Positive reinforcements for desirable behavior will vary. I recommend things like praise, encouragement, and experiences rather than toys or food. But what matters most is consistency. Provide positive reinforcement whenever your child performs a behavior that you're targeting. If you're working on clearing the dishes after meals, praise your child the moment you notice them doing it: "Great job clearing your dishes!" Many of the behaviors you're cultivating are hard for your kid, so it's important to recognize their efforts even when they don't complete an action fully. If they clear their plate but not their fork, that's still progress. Catching them doing well at small changes leads to bigger changes over time.

Reinforcement in Action

During graduate school, I completed a year of clinical training at an intensive program for at-risk children with severe behavioral problems. The clinical staff's approach was to recognize and encourage the clients when they engaged in appropriate behaviors, while also providing them guidance, structure, and skills. By the end of the year, I was amazed at the changes I saw in many of the children, most of them the result of reinforcement.

While there, I worked with a young boy from a troubled family. His behavioral problems had put him at risk for expulsion from school, and his future seemed bleak. Sadly, he was accustomed to relating to adults through punishment and scolding, but I saw changes in him soon after he started the program. When we did things as simple as praising him for following directions the first time he was asked, his behavior began to shift. He liked being noticed for doing well rather than for messing up. Suddenly, his true personality shone through, and he could engage with the world in healthier ways. Although positive reinforcement isn't the only reason he made such incredible gains, it played a pivotal role.

Don't Punish, Extinguish

If reducing punishment is the goal, what should you do instead? *Extinction*, or ignoring unwanted behaviors, is a very effective strategy. If, for example, your child is whining about wanting a new toy at the store, rather than scold them, you'd simply ignore them. Scolding inadvertently rewards the whining with attention, but if you ignore the whining, your child will learn over time that it won't get them what they desire. I know this one is hard! Fortunately, when paired with positive reinforcement of desirable behaviors, it's a very powerful tool. Let's go over how to effectively extinguish behaviors in more detail.

Extinction is the lack of an expected reinforcement for a behavior. Like punishment, on its own extinction isn't the best way to shape behavior, because it doesn't guide your child's actions toward more appropriate responses. That's why this program pairs extinction with positive reinforcement. If, for example, your teenager complains that you don't let them use the car enough, you'd ignore their complaints—but if they ask politely, you could positively reinforce their request by remarking that they asked very maturely. You could even reward them for asking so appropriately by letting them use the car. Next time they want to use the car, they'll likely remember how asking worked better than complaining. This is an effective use of extinction coupled with positive reinforcement.

Many of us grew up with the notion that punishment is a necessary component of parenting, and there are certain times when it will be called for. However, for the vast majority of children with ODD, punishment is highly *in*effective. These kids have great difficulty with authority, so when a parent tries to instill greater compliance through punishment, the child will almost always rebel. This leads to a vicious cycle of increased defiance in reaction to increased punishment and control. In their book *Alternatives to Punishment*, Gary LaVigna and Anne Donnellan write that one of the main reasons reinforcement strategies are more effective than punishment is that punishment tends to increase negative feelings in both the child and the parent. When was the last time you were punished by an authority figure and felt good about it?

Another problem with punishment is that it teaches the child only what behaviors *not* to do. Children with ODD need help learning what behaviors *to do*. Remember, kids with ODD have skills deficits. Part of helping them manage their ODD is teaching them new skills. If you punish your child by taking away their favorite toy when they talk back to you, it might teach them not to talk back—but likely not for very long, because that's not the lesson they really need to learn. Instead, they need to learn how to manage their frustration better and speak respectfully to others. Taking away the toy teaches neither.

Note that when extinction is first introduced, a phenomenon known as an "extinction burst" may occur. This is essentially a temporary increase in the problematic behavior as your child tries to figure out how to get the desired reaction from you. This can cause many parents to throw in the towel and declare that extinction is the worst tool ever! I urge you to stay the course, work on your own self-calming strategies, and stick to the plan. Extinction bursts are temporary as long as you don't give in. Again, consistency is essential.

Extinction in Action

A good example of extinction in action is an adolescent client of mine, Jazmine, who struggled with managing her intense emotions when she didn't get her way. She had aggressive tantrums well past the age that most children do, and her parents would give in to her to avoid the eruption. But after a few sessions, her parents began to institute an extinction procedure. During Jazmine's next tantrum, their homework assignment was to say, "When you're ready to speak calmly to me, I'll listen." If Jazmine persisted, they were to calmly

Extinction

Below is a sample dialogue between a parent and their ten-year-old child, using extinction and positive reinforcement. Consider how to incorporate these skills into your toolbox.

Parent: Time to take out the trash.

Child: (Beginning to cry) No! You do it! I don't want to!

Parent: I can't understand you when you raise your voice. When you're ready to talk in a lower voice, I'll be here.

Child: (Crying and yelling) That's stupid! I'm not taking out the trash!

Parent: (Ignores the behavior)

Child: I'm not doing it! It's not my trash!

Parent: (Ignores the behavior)

Child: (Starting to remove the trash bag) This is so dumb! Why do I have to do all the work?

Parent: I know you're mad, and I appreciate your helping out.

Child: (Calmer voice, still tearful) It's so unfair!

Parent: I hear you. You feel it's unfair, and you're still helping out. Thank you.

In this conversation, the parent held firm and stayed calm. When the child changed their behavior, the parent reinforced it by praising and validating them. Like all skills, this takes some practice, but you can do it!

repeat the phrase and nothing else. The moment Jazmine began to respond appropriately, they'd make a quick statement of praise and then attend to her.

Initially, Jazmine, who was used to getting her way, persisted, sometimes for over an hour. It was tiring, but her parents held their ground. Eventually, Jazmine would get fed up and calmly make her request. The extended outbursts happened a few more times, but within three weeks, they became less intense and shorter in duration. When we all debriefed in a family session, Jazmine reported she was "sick of hearing my parents say the same thing over and over." Though it takes time to adjust to, extinction can work wonders in changing your child's unhelpful habits.

Alternative Behaviors: What Should They Do Instead?

When parents first meet with me, they usually have a laundry list of their child's difficult behaviors that they want to eradicate—screaming, cussing, disobeying, throwing things, hitting, talking back to teachers. After listening to the list of the things they want their child to *stop* doing, I ask a follow-up question: "What do you want them to *start* doing instead?" Almost always, they say, "I want them to stop doing those things." Of course these behaviors cause serious problems at home and at school, so it's not surprising that they're foremost in parents' minds. But until they can reasonably identify what they want their kid to do instead, we won't get very far.

When it comes to behavior change, we can't really take something away without adding something in its place. You wouldn't expect your toddler to go straight from diapers to using the toilet without first teaching them how to use it. Even after you taught them, you likely expected them to have accidents until they got the hang of potty training. You provided your child with a new option for going to the bathroom, *and* you helped them gain the skills to recognize when and how to use the toilet. In the same way, you can't expect your child to just stop doing a disruptive or defiant behavior because you told them so. Instead, you'll need to figure out which behaviors you want to replace the unhelpful ones.

I had a client who was really sassy to adults, engaging in a lot of backtalk even with grown-ups she didn't know. With some guidance, her parents were able to set a concrete goal of speaking respectfully to adults rather than talking back. Suddenly, there was a behavior that they could positively reinforce while extinguishing the sass.

Saying "No" Isn't Enough

If you're like many parents today, you grew up in a household where phrases like, "I said no, that's why," and, "Because I said so," were standard parental responses to children's questions. This may have worked on you and your siblings, but I guarantee it won't work for your child with ODD, because such responses trigger their defiance and oppositional behavior. The more an ODD kid feels controlled, the more defiance will emerge.

You know from chapter 2 that once triggered, it's really hard for your child to behave appropriately. Saying no to a behavior without providing an alternative shuts down problem-solving, leaving your child stuck with their difficult thoughts and feelings. Providing alternative options, on the other hand, allows your child to gain new skills and manage their intense feelings adaptively.

Note that this doesn't mean rewarding your child for their "bad" behavior. Parents often mistakenly believe that the only way to discipline a child is to punish them and that if they don't, the child will run amok. But ODD kids' behavioral problems are usually already wreaking havoc on the home, even with strict rules and heavy punishments. When parents respond by making the rules even more stringent, it only exacerbates their child's defiance. The goal of this book is to stop this harmful, exhausting, and ineffective cycle and replace it with habits that work.

The word *discipline* has become associated with punishment, but it originates from the Latin *disciplina*, which translates to "instruction" or "knowledge." In your efforts to help your child manage their ODD symptoms, can you learn to think of discipline as a means of instructing them or giving them knowledge of new, more effective tools? If so, I'm confident you'll have better results.

Alternative Behaviors in Action

When I was training in community mental health, I worked with a child, Tobias, who had extreme behavioral problems. They were so severe he had to be homeschooled because he refused to go to class, and when he did he'd cause a ruckus. He was aggressive, argumentative, and abusive toward his siblings and harbored a great deal of anger and anxiety.

There were lots of other familial stressors going on in the home, and Tobias's parents were worn out. They'd established a complex set of rules and punishments to coerce him into obedience, but the stricter the rules, the greater his defiance. One thing they punished him for was his frequent complaining. After a few sessions, I gently nudged them to lay off the punishments and asked what behaviors they wanted to see him engage in instead. Both said they hoped he would express his frustration in more productive ways.

We discussed possible alternatives, and they landed on encouraging him to express what he *did* want rather than what he didn't. Whenever he chose to use more assertive communication instead of complaining, they positively reinforced him. Within weeks, the number of complaints per day had decreased. Tobias's parents were amazed that they didn't need to use punishment to accomplish their goal. Though they still had a long way to go, this was a successful first step in shaping their child's behavior for the better.

Parent-Child Exercise

This exercise will let you practice positive reinforcement while joining your child in a fun activity. It's much easier to practice these skills when things are going well, so get your child's input on what activity they'd like to do. I'd suggest a board game, playing catch, cooking, or anything that doesn't involve TV or video games. Make sure you're fully focused on the task—no checking email or multitasking.

During the activity, notice when your child does things you want them to do more of, and then make encouraging comments or give them praise. This helps shape their behavior and teaches them what you want them to do. Keep in mind, your praise should be sincere. For example, if you're playing Uno and your child appears to be really concentrating on their strategy, you can say, "It looks like you're really focused." If you're making a meal, you could comment, "I notice you're measuring very carefully." See how they respond to your encouragement and how many times you can *catch them doing well*.

At the end of the activity, check in with one another on how each of you thought the activity went. This is one step toward connecting with your child through positive behavior shaping.

Boundaries: How to Set Them, How to Keep Them

Now that you have a better understanding of how to use consequences and alternatives with your child, we'll focus on how to set healthy boundaries. I saved this for last because consequences and alternatives play a key role in boundary setting. As you may remember, boundaries are limits, rules, and expectations for behavior. Children with ODD, by definition, struggle to respect appropriate boundaries, not because they're mean or bad but because they don't yet have the right tools to navigate social situations.

As with alternative behaviors, when it comes to creating boundaries, it's more important to figure out what you *do* want instead of what you *don't* want. If you want to reduce things like yelling, screaming, and name-calling in your home, good boundaries might be, "We speak to one another with respect and kindness," and, "We use a calm voice when we talk." Setting clear and healthy expectations for how you treat each other is essential not only for your ODD child but for all members of your household.

Of course, setting boundaries is the easy part. Consistently enforcing them can be quite hard! Children in general tend to push boundaries—it's a normal part of development. They're trying to figure out how important the rules are, which ones you'll actually enforce, and which you'll let slide. Children with ODD often smash through any and all boundaries because they get so caught up in their intense feelings that they basically disregard everything else.

Maintaining the boundaries you and your family set will be a full-time job. You see, boundaries are only effective if you consistently keep them. If you don't, you'll teach your child that the more they persist with their defiance, aggression, or whining, the more likely you'll be to relent. This doesn't just reinforce but actually escalates the very behaviors you wish to see changed. This is true of all children, but especially those with ODD, who already dislike and challenge authority. They'll test every boundary you set, even the ones they themselves came up with. Since change is hard, they'll try to push you to go back to the old way of doing things. However, you now know better and have an arsenal of skills to make maintaining limits more realistic. Stay strong!

Keeping the boundaries you set will require a lot of the self-care tools we discussed in part 1 of this book. You'll need to work on managing your triggers and increasing your compassion for yourself and your child. If you find yourself struggling to maintain your boundaries, spend some time taking care of you. It'll give you the strength to stay firm. Also, don't forget to give yourself some grace—all of this is new to you, and you'll make mistakes. The goal is not perfection but consistency.

Collaborate to Set Expectations

Like most of us, kids like to have input about the rules and expectations set for them. Collaborating with your children on new limits you decide to set is a great way to get them to "sign off" on the new program and gives them a feeling of investment in the process. There are certain boundaries they won't like, and that's okay. Your child may never like weekend chores, and your tween likely hates that there's a limit on screen time. This is part of ordinary family life. Still, being open to hearing their thoughts and feelings on the subject can buy you a lot of goodwill. Often, children just want to feel understood.

In areas where there's room for negotiation, invite your child to come up with suggestions. For example, if they want a later bedtime, find out how they plan to manage getting less sleep. If there's wiggle room, can you help them come up with a plan to satisfy you both? In this case, you might allow them to stay up thirty minutes later, as long as they can still get up on time the following day. If they can't keep their end of the bargain, then it's time to reevaluate. The purpose of setting boundaries isn't to gain more control but to increase harmony, safety, and respect. Collaboration can help accomplish that.

Boundaries: Examples

Boundaries is a broad term, so here are a few examples to get you thinking about what appropriate boundaries will look like in your family.

- José struggles with completing his chores, so his parents set the expectation that he can watch television once he's completed his daily chores.

- Sixteen-year-old Ryann would like her curfew extended until midnight. A new boundary allows her to stay out until midnight if she's at an organized activity/event.
- Noah is eight and hates vegetables but loves dessert. The limit becomes that once he eats his serving of veggies at dinner, he's allowed to have a small treat for dessert.
- Amaya has tantrums and talks back when her parents don't buy her a toy on trips to the store. Each time she doesn't have a tantrum at the store, her parents give her a coupon that she can save until she has enough to earn an agreed-upon reward.
- Marie picks on her little sister constantly. Her parents establish the rule, "We treat each other with kindness." When they catch Marie being kind to her sister, they encourage her behavior.

These are just a few examples of how you could put boundary setting into action in your family. Remember, you'll have more success if you make this a collaborative process with your child.

Action Plan: Target Positive Behaviors for Reinforcement

Over the next week, your assignment is to target some positive or desirable behaviors for reinforcement. The purpose of the task is to catch your child doing well! Here's a three-step action plan.

1. Identify two behaviors you want your child to do. You can use the problematic behaviors identified in the chapter 5 action plan or come up with new ones. Be specific—for example, "managing frustration without throwing things" or "beginning homework the first time they're asked." You could even get your child's input on the changes *they* want to work on.
2. Each time your child engages in these desired behaviors, praise them. If they pull out their notebook after you've asked them to

get started on their homework, compliment them for being such a good listener. Be genuine in your encouragement.

3. At the end of the week, reflect on whether your child's behavior has started to change with the reinforcement. If it hasn't, notice if they're making partial attempts that have gone unnoticed. Sometimes they don't quite have the skill set to complete tasks as expected and need encouragement to make partial attempts complete.

Takeaways

- Alternatives, boundaries, and consequences are the ABCs of your ODD toolbox.
- *Alternatives* are new behaviors and skills your child can use instead of old unhelpful ones.
- *Boundaries* are limits and expectations for behavior.
- *Consequences* are the result of a person's actions (positive, negative, or neutral) and are not the same as punishment.
- Punishment tends to be more harmful than helpful and does not teach new skills.
- Extinguish unwanted behaviors by ignoring them whenever possible and positively reinforcing desired behaviors instead.
- Positive reinforcement is an effective way to help your child change their behavior for the better.
- Figuring out what behaviors you'd like to see your child do is more helpful than focusing on what you *don't* want them to do.

CHAPTER SEVEN

Putting Your Tools to Work: Three Steps to Change

Your Tools: An Overview

The previous chapter provided important tools for helping you guide your child to manage their ODD symptoms more adaptively. As you recall, we focused on the ABCs: alternatives, boundaries, and consequences. Below is a brief overview of the ABCs as a quick refresher before we jump into examples and exercises.

Alternatives are helpful skills and behaviors that children with ODD can use instead of unhelpful ones. Because these kids usually have limited problem-solving skills and don't know what appropriate behaviors to use, providing other options is key. I had a client named Xavier who struggled with managing his anger and had outbursts that included throwing toys at family members and peers. His parents began to present him with alternatives when he'd get mad, such as throwing a foam ball at the wall. This was the first step in helping him learn to direct his anger away from others while still expressing it. The alternatives were modified as he became better able to manage his emotions. Soon, he had learned to "take five" when his feelings of anger exceeded a level three. Providing your child with alternatives will let you mold their behavior by giving them new skills and choices.

Boundaries are limits, expectations, and rules. Children with ODD often resist boundaries, though they need them even more than most kids due to their skills deficits. Boundaries allow children (and adults) to know what's expected regarding how they treat others and how others treat them. One family I worked with had very few limits or rules. The father had grown up in an authoritarian, punitive household, and, not wanting to repeat his parents' mistake, he didn't set limits for his own children. His daughter, Julie, had become increasingly defiant and argumentative, which he didn't realize was in response to the household's lack of structure; Julie felt like she needed to be in charge, since her parents didn't seem to be. I immediately worked with the father to start setting limits. Though Julie initially pushed back, she eventually began to respect the boundaries, and her anxiety and defiance went down. Children, especially those with ODD, have difficulty anticipating the consequences of their actions. Having clear and consistent limits can teach them the relationship between their actions and what happens as a result, which will be useful as you work to change their behavior.

Consequences are the results—positive, negative, or neutral—of a behavior or action. You can use them to guide your child's behavior in healthy ways. While there may be times when it's necessary to implement a punishment, positive reinforcement will be the most common consequence used in this work; research shows that it's more effective than punishment in shaping behavior. Besides, there's a good chance you've already gone the punishment route with your child and it didn't work. When I counseled the family of a three-year-old boy on creating consequences, the parents were amazed at how much he could do on his own when given the opportunity to earn a reward rather than a punishment. Consequences can help your child grow in confidence and internal motivation, thereby increasing their ability to do well.

Now that we've reviewed the ABCs, we're ready to jump in and put them to work. Keep in mind that the changes you're setting out to make for your child are positive, and they are also hard. If you're struggling with this, you're normal. Don't give up.

Creating Consequences

Let's take a closer look at how you can effectively use consequences with your child. As you read this section, think about ways to incorporate these skills into your parenting.

Punishment: When and Why

Let's start with the elephant in the room. We've talked about how punishment is not as effective as positive reinforcement but may *sometimes* be necessary to shape your child's behavior in appropriate ways. Those times include instances when your child's behavior poses a safety issue or when they deliberately break a reasonable expectation with no sign of accepting responsibility. For example, if your teen drinks alcohol and then drives, it's reasonable to revoke their driving privileges for a period because drinking and driving is a safety issue. Or if your child purposely injures a kid at school and defends their actions without accepting responsibility, a punishment *may* be needed. When you do punish your child, it's helpful to remain calm, firm, and consistent and refrain from hitting or spanking. You can't teach your child to reduce their aggression by directing aggression at them.

Positive Reinforcement Goes a Long Way

Consider which of your child's behaviors need the most urgent attention. If you're stumped, start with safety concerns—your child's or someone else's. For example, my son hates wearing his helmet when he rides his scooter. After my threats to take away his scooter (which would have been a punishment) found little success, I rebranded scooter riding as a *reward* for wearing his helmet: "If you wear your helmet, you get to ride your scooter." It worked, not because he's a super compliant child but because he loves riding his scooter, and wearing a helmet gets him what he wants.

The number one complaint that comes up with my clients is screen time (time on phones, computers, TV, etc.). Children and adolescents always want more while parents think they already have too much. If you make screen time a reward for appropriate behaviors, rather than threatening to take it away as a punishment, then you'll increase the likelihood that your child does something you want them to do in order to earn it. For example, if you want your child to begin their homework right after school, you can offer them an extra five minutes of screen time once they've completed their work. Suddenly, you're on their side and not the person standing between them and their precious device.

Example: Emotional Volatility

Children with ODD are emotionally volatile, going from calm to full-blown tantrum mode in a heartbeat. Since you already know this is related to skills deficits in emotion regulation, you can use consequences to help increase their ability to manage their intense feelings in healthy ways.

During my clinical training, I was assigned to a program that provided therapy to children in their homes. Children were eligible for these intensive services because they had extreme behavioral problems that caused them significant impairment at home, at school, and with their peers. One of my clients, Anand, was prone to severe, increasingly violent emotional fits. Though he was only in middle school, the police had come to his home on several occasions because he'd threatened his parents.

In an attempt to manage his behavior, Anand's parents became highly punitive, but the more punishments he earned, the more upset he'd get, and his behaviors only escalated. He had no fear of authority, which most adults interpreted as disrespect. After a few sessions, it became apparent he *did* respect his parents and teachers—he just didn't know any other way to handle feelings of rejection, shame, and sadness that arose when he made a mistake.

His parents and I worked together to focus on helping him express his feelings in healthy ways, whether he was excited about a playdate or angry he got picked last for kickball. Every time he appropriately expressed his feelings, he was praised and encouraged. His parents created a point system: He earned two points every time he identified a feeling and five points each time he caught himself before he had a tantrum. The points were tied to rewards like playing a game with his dad. After several months, he had learned the skills to manage his feelings more adaptively, not through punishment but through the careful cultivation of alternative behaviors that gave him the skills he needed.

What skills could your child improve on when it comes to emotional reactivity? Start thinking of ways you can positively reinforce them with praise or encouragement. Remember, big changes start small.

Action Step #1: Emotional Volatility

In this chapter, we'll use three "action steps" to create a treatment plan to help with the three big trouble spots of ODD: emotional volatility, inflexibility, and defiance of authority. Keep in mind that you shouldn't institute too many changes at once. I suggest targeting no more than one behavior every week or two. If you try to institute them too quickly, it will lead to frustration and failure.

Action step #1 will focus on reducing your child's emotional volatility. Using your notebook and/or calendar, complete the following tasks:

1. **Identify the target behavior.** Think about where your child struggles most with managing their emotions. Be as specific as possible. ("My child has a fit when asked to do chores.") Next, consider what behavior you'd like them to do *instead*. ("I want them to express their anger in safe and respectful ways.") Feel free to use your work from the action plans in chapters 5 and 6.

2. **Set a SMART goal related to the target behavior.** A SMART goal is specific, measurable, attainable, realistic, and time-sensitive. For instance, "My child will use at least one helpful behavior (identifying feelings, taking space, deep breathing) to express their anger within two weeks." Start small—this is one step toward the larger goal of communicating anger appropriately.

3. **Use the ABCs.** Write down some alternative behaviors that could help your child manage and communicate their feelings, like asking for space or doing deep-breathing exercises. Next, list some realistic boundaries you can set, such as, "It's okay to be angry, but it's not okay to scream." Then consider how you can create positive consequences like praise for actions aligned with the alternative behavior. Collaborating with your child on which rewards to use

Remember to Take Care of You

You're doing some heavy lifting right now! By this point, you've learned lots of tools and are beginning to implement them in specific ways, all while managing the daily stressors of having a child with ODD. Have you kept up your self-care routine? Because that is essential to your success.

If you've slacked a bit here, I understand. Self-care is usually the first thing busy parents let slide. This is another friendly reminder that taking care of yourself is part of your child's treatment plan.

In case you need a few ideas, here are some easy, practical ways to refresh and rejuvenate:

- *Meditate*
- *Listen to a favorite song or podcast*
- *Breathe deeply for two minutes*
- *Call a friend*
- *Go on a walk*
- *Pet a furry friend*
- *Pray*
- *Color or sketch*
- *Do a craft*
- *Spend time with a spouse/partner*
- *Take a bath*
- *Look at old photos*

Whatever it is that brings you joy, relaxation, or peace—even just for two minutes—counts as self-care. Ideally, you can do something for yourself daily. It's not about how much time you spend but how intentionally you make yourself a priority.

(stickers, extra playtime) when they express their anger respectfully is also a good strategy.

4. **Track progress.** Keep track of your child's progress by logging it in your notebook/calendar. If they're having fewer outbursts when angry or complying the second time they're asked to do something, write that down. Positively reinforce even partial successes or attempts; any step in the right direction is progress. Once your child has met the goal, increase it slightly. ("My child will use *three* helpful behaviors to express their anger within two weeks.") Monitoring progress will give you a more realistic view of their growth.

Identifying Alternatives

Helping parents and children identify healthy alternative behaviors is one of the most gratifying parts of my work as a child psychologist. Learning new skills increases a child's ability to navigate life successfully. Since children with ODD have skills deficits in emotion regulation, social skills, and executive functioning, they're in desperate need of these tools.

Consider what skills your child needs to learn in order to behave in appropriate ways. The goal is not to focus on what they shouldn't do but to build up their ability to use more desirable behaviors. If they seem to have problems with kids at school because they constantly interrupt, then they could probably use some help with social skills and impulse control. You can practice having conversations with your child, review the basic aspects of a conversation, and praise them when you notice even the smallest reduction in interruptions.

Children with ODD have lots of difficulty with intense feelings. It can be helpful to create a list of options for them to use when they start feeling out of control. Ideally, these options could be done anywhere, like deep breathing, labeling/rating feelings, or doing 20 jumping jacks. The purpose of identifying alternatives is to give your child something to do instead of their problematic behavior. Over time, they'll grow to understand that problems can be solved in many different ways.

Example: Inflexibility

Flexibility can be challenging for anyone, but it's especially difficult for children who don't yet have the skills to manage their emotions. Whenever I see inflexibility, I immediately assess for anxiety symptoms. Anxious thinking tells us we need to be 100 percent certain about what will happen to us in order to be safe. This means that people prone to anxiety can really struggle with, for example, sudden changes of plan or the transition from a familiar environment (school) to a new one (a museum field trip).

I worked with a seven-year-old girl named Lucia who was highly oppositional, especially when confronted with change. If there was a substitute teacher at school, she'd throw a violent fit. At home, she'd resist even the slightest shift from the status quo, even to do things she usually found enjoyable. This made a certain amount of sense because she'd undergone a big, traumatic change: Her mother had died when she was just four years old. Her dad, a single father, was at a loss about how to handle his daughter's frequent outbursts.

I worked with Lucia on skills to understand her emotions and thoughts while simultaneously working with her father on identifying alternatives she could use when triggered. Initially, it was challenging because her level of volatility was so high. Within weeks, though, her dad became better at anticipating her tantrums early. He then gave her several options for coping, including taking a pause, sharing her feelings and thoughts, and playing on her iPad for a few minutes as a distraction.

Though she needed a lot of guidance toward the new behaviors at first, she slowly started using them more often on her own, and her dad positively reinforced her when she did. Within six months, she was much less defiant, and her tantrums at home and school were reduced by about 75 percent. She also had much more confidence in her ability to cope with life because of her new skills.

Consider what it would be like if you could help your child to have significantly fewer ODD symptoms. The ABCs give you the skills to help your child thrive.

Action Step #2: Inflexibility

Action step #2 will focus on helping your child become more flexible using the ABCs. This is the second goal in your treatment plan. You'll notice that the exercises are the same as in action step #1, but this time with examples related to inflexibility.

Complete the following tasks in your notebook and/or calendar:

1. **Identify the target behavior.** How does your child's inflexibility negatively impact them most? (Feel free to use your work from the action plans in chapters 5 and 6.) For many kids, inflexibility comes to a head during transitions because it's hard for them to switch from one mind-set to another. A good example is a child who becomes aggressive when told to prepare for bed. The target behavior would be to increase peaceful transitions at bedtime.

2. **Set a SMART goal related to the target behavior.** A SMART goal is specific, measurable, attainable, realistic, and time-sensitive. An example for the above target behavior might be, "My child will willingly go to bed within 10 minutes of their bedtime once in the next week."

3. **Use the ABCs.** Write down some alternative behaviors that you could introduce to help your child increase their flexibility, such as a 30-minute countdown to prepare them for bedtime or a 10-minute grace period. Next, collaborate on boundaries; perhaps there's a set bedtime on weekdays, but they can stay up an hour later on weekends. Now identify the positive consequences you'll use to reinforce progress—perhaps a sticker chart for younger kids or extra privileges for older kids.

4. **Track progress.** Don't forget to keep track of your child's progress in your notebook/calendar so you don't overlook their previous successes when they're going through a rough patch. Seeing their improvement in writing helps you keep things in perspective.

Setting Boundaries

Imagine if your boss told you she wanted to work with you to come up with reasonable and effective expectations to help you reach your performance goals. Wouldn't you be more inclined to respect those expectations since you had a voice in creating them? Your child is no different. They want to succeed, too. Collaboration and realistic boundary setting can help them grow.

Think of this work as a fresh start for you and your child. It's an opportunity to intentionally create new limits and expectations that are aligned with your parenting values and goals. If you want your children to grow up to be self-motivated, hardworking, helpful, and respectful to others, come up with boundaries that will move your household closer to those goals. It may be that you focus on rules surrounding how you treat one another and forgo harping on your child for messiness, because you feel being respectful is a greater priority. You can always come back to less important expectations later, but right now you have bigger fish to fry.

Are there any rules you can eliminate because they're low priority, too rigid, or ineffective? I worked with one parent who insisted her teenager wash his bedsheets every week, which became a huge power struggle and led to blowout arguments. When I asked why this was so important, she said she wanted her child to sleep in a clean bed. After some discussion, she decided she preferred to live in harmony with her child, even if that meant stinky sheets. She chose to lay down her half of the rope, and that game of tug-of-war ended. Though children with ODD need structure and clear expectations, being overly rule-based only exacerbates their defiance.

Picture your child's surprise when you tell them you're going to do away with some rules! It will demonstrate your willingness to be flexible and help foster collaborative discussions about boundaries and why they're important.

Example: Defiance of Authority

I truly believe that defiance symptoms are very treatable for the majority of children with ODD. Given consistent and clear boundaries, solid coping skills, and lots of patience, these children can usually thrive, no matter how defiant they are initially.

I once worked with a seventeen-year-old client named Malik who was outrageously defiant toward adults. He was referred to me because of an escalation in behaviors that included cussing out a clergy member, the school principal, and a police officer, all within three weeks. Needless to say, he wasn't excited to see me. He threatened to walk out of the first two sessions because he felt I was wasting his time.

Fortunately, he didn't—probably more because of the huge bowl of chocolates in my office than because of my therapeutic prowess—and eventually he opened up about his feelings. It turned out Malik felt bad about himself. His behavior was so egregious that kids at school wanted nothing to do with him, and he came to believe his only value was to play the role of rebel. He thought his parents had written him off as a lost cause, and in certain ways they had. With his eighteenth birthday approaching, he feared they'd follow through with their threats to kick him out of the house. He didn't see much value in making any changes.

I conducted several family therapy sessions with Malik and his parents. We focused on creating opportunities for him to succeed, which included eliminating half the rules that had been established to force him into compliance. He no longer had to make his bed every morning or go to sleep by 10:30 on weeknights, but we retained more important rules like curfew and daily school attendance. The family worked together on establishing boundaries for how they treated each other—it turns out Malik wasn't the only one in the house who cussed people out. "Everyone deserves to be spoken to respectfully," became a new rule.

Two months into treatment, Malik began to tear up in session. He reported his dad had recently gotten mad at him for not taking the garbage cans out on trash day. Usually his dad would berate him and call him a loser. However, this time, when his dad began to yell, he caught himself and apologized. This deeply moved Malik. Though it wasn't completely perfect, his dad had observed the boundary of respect. This became a catalyst for change for Malik. Though it took about a year, he was able to learn the skills he needed to manage his emotions and impulsivity more adaptively. In time, you can be that catalyst for change for your child!

Action Step #3: Defiance of Authority

Now you're on to action step #3 in your child's treatment plan. Again, you can refer back to your action plan from chapter 5 or come up with new behaviors to target.

Complete the following tasks in your notebook and/or calendar:

1. **Identify the target behavior.** How does your child's defiance get in their way? Be as specific as possible, using your action plans from chapters 5 and 6 if desired. Many children with ODD talk back to their parents in the mistaken belief that they have equal authority. A target behavior may be that you want your child to respect your authority as parent.

2. **Set a SMART goal for the target behavior.** SMART stands for specific, measurable, attainable, realistic, and time-sensitive. A SMART goal for the above target behavior might be, "My child will follow directions on two tasks the first time asked within two weeks."

3. **Use the ABCs.** Write down some alternative behaviors you could introduce to help your child follow directions more readily, such as expressing their frustration respectfully before doing the task or

giving them a five-minute window to start the task. Next, collaborate on boundaries related to following directives; you could both agree to be respectful in giving directives and following them, even if frustrated. Now, identify positive consequences you'll use to reinforce progress, like praise, thanks, or extra privileges. Recall the power of extinguishing negative behaviors by ignoring them whenever possible!

4. **Track progress.** Don't forget to keep track of your child's progress in your notebook/calendar. You don't want to overlook their overall progress when they have a bad day. As they improve their skills, you can target new behaviors to keep that progress going.

Now you have your three targeted behavioral goals, which means you have a treatment plan that is custom tailored to your child's needs. Great work!

Action Plan: One-Week Intervention for Target Behavior

Congratulations! You've created the initial treatment plan for your child! I know this chapter has been a lot of work and likely took up a good chunk of time.

Now that you have that plan, let's map out how you'll begin to use it. Present the treatment plan to your child, explaining that it's intended to help you provide tools and skills to help them succeed. Talk to them about your responsibilities as well (self-care, consistency, maintaining boundaries, etc.). Answer any questions, and focus on this being a positive process, not a punitive one. Collaborate as much as possible, and seek feedback regarding boundaries and positive consequences. You may find they're excited about the change!

I highly recommend focusing on one action step at a time and spending at least one to two weeks (possibly more) on each goal individually. Don't forget to track progress so you know when it's time to move on to another goal or to increase expectations for the current goal. This, of course, will depend on your child's participation and your consistency. It's not unusual for progress to go slowly at first while everyone adjusts to the new program.

If you get stumped, go back to your ABCs. Don't be afraid to identify more alternatives and increase the positive reinforcement and extinguishing (ignoring). Don't jump to other goals until your child has completed the initial goal. And once you've completed all the action steps, set new ones. Your child's treatment plan will continuously evolve until they show a marked reduction in ODD symptoms.

Takeaways

- You've gained several tools to help your child.
- SMART goals are specific, measurable, attainable, realistic, and time-sensitive.
- Action steps have four parts: targeting a behavior, creating a SMART goal, using the ABCs, and tracking progress.
- Together, the action steps form a treatment plan to help your child learn to manage their ODD.
- Remember your own self-care.
- Make sure your child has reached a goal before starting on the next one.
- If you get stumped, try changing some of the ABCs—just let your child know if you're changing a boundary.
- Notice, praise, and encourage any progress, even if it's an incomplete attempt.
- Stay consistent, remain patient, and be hopeful!

CHAPTER EIGHT

Managing Extreme Behaviors

Dealing with Severe Symptoms

Now that you've created a working treatment plan, let's look at how you can help your child manage their most difficult behaviors. I've worked with many ODD kids, and some of my favorite clients have been the ones with the most intense symptoms. I can connect with them because I'm not afraid of their roars and prickliness; I understand the role those behaviors play in helping these kids get by. I've learned to look beyond the hard exterior to see the vulnerable child underneath, lacking adequate skills but brimming with possibility. Similarly, I've sat with parents as they've wept with fear and frustration and seen them find new hope for their child as they learn skills to pass on. I sincerely believe that this chapter will give you practical, effective tools to help you feel more confident in your ability to effect true change in your child's life.

The diagnostic criteria for ODD include angry/irritable mood, argumentative/defiant behavior, and vindictiveness that cause significant impairment in functioning. These symptoms range from mild to severe. In their most severe form, they can become downright dangerous. If you feel that many, even most, of your child's behaviors are extreme, that's normal for parents in your situation. ODD is characterized by *externalizing behaviors*—lashing out reactively rather than moderating intense feelings. This means that your child's day-to-day reactions to fear or frustration probably seem far more extreme than the run-of-the-mill defiance and sassiness you see in other children.

In this chapter, the extreme behaviors I'll focus on will be violence, psychological abuse, and acting out in public places. I'm sure you have battle stories about enduring public tantrums, physical aggression, and verbal assaults at the hands of your child. Let's work on some tools to help you and your child learn better ways of managing.

Keep Your Cool

Perhaps you rolled your eyes when you read this section's title. I probably would, too, if I were you. Keeping your cool is easier said than done during one of your child's eruptions, which might include screaming, punching, name-calling, and other forms of aggression. Trying to remain calm when your child is being verbally or physically aggressive toward you, others, or themselves is no easy task. Still, there's great power in learning to manage your own heightened emotions when your child is spiraling out of control. This all goes back to part 1 of this book and the skills you learned to break the reactivity cycle. Remember, when you get upset in response to your child's strong emotions, it only escalates their reaction. It might be helpful to reread chapters 2 and 3 as you work through tackling some of the more extreme behaviors your child exhibits.

I was recently in a grocery store when I heard a child having a meltdown in the canned goods aisle. Though I've seen plenty of kids throwing public tantrums, I've rarely seen a calm parent accompanying them. But this girl's father was the picture of patience. He didn't try to force her off the ground or stop her response. Rather, he stood there patiently, and when she'd get too near the shelf, he'd calmly say, "Careful, I don't want you to get hurt." A couple times, he asked if she needed a hug. Within a few minutes, the weeping, shrieking child was in his arms and on the road to emotion regulation. He was able to manage his emotions in such a way that he helped his daughter regulate hers.

Author L. R. Knost noted, "When little people are overwhelmed by big emotions, it's our job to share our calm, not to join their chaos." We can't help our children manage their emotional volatility if we can't manage ours. That's why learning tools to cope with their outbursts is such a necessary part of this work.

There will be times when your child acts out so forcefully that it'll feel impossible *not* to react, even with your new skills. When you have those reactive moments yourself, remember it's par for the course, and have some compassion for yourself and the hard work you're doing. Try some strategies from part 1 of this book, like deep breathing for two minutes, listening to a guided meditation, or taking a pause. Attending to your emotional well-being in those moments will help you choose your next steps more successfully.

Maintain Consistency

In order to effectively assist your child with managing their extreme behaviors, you'll need to remain consistent with your ABCs. It may feel like I'm asking you to do two impossible tasks—remain calm and maintain consistency—when doing just one of them can require almost superhuman strength. But remember, you now have critical knowledge and tools to face these challenges.

All kids need consistency. Children with ODD need it even more urgently than their peers due to their internal chaos and frequent emotional upset. Your stability and predictability will let them feel safe because they'll know what to expect and what's expected of them. Keeping changes small but consistent is key to maintaining boundaries and implementing consequences. Though it may feel like change is slow, that consistency increases your chance of creating lasting change over time.

If you're finding consistency difficult, review the skills in chapters 2 and 3. Mindfulness can help you calm yourself while distress-tolerance skills let you manage your own discomfort when your child's defiance and aggression are at their peak. It's 100 percent okay to feel angry, disappointed, overwhelmed, embarrassed, sad, or any other feeling, as long as you express those emotions in healthy ways. Again, this will take work and a lot of self-compassion.

Violence

Now that we've established the importance of remaining calm and consistent when managing your child's extreme behaviors, let's identify interventions, or tools, to reduce the frequency, intensity, and duration of these episodes. Before we begin, I want to give an important disclaimer: If your child's extreme behaviors pose an immediate danger to themselves or others, please call 911 or take them to the nearest emergency room. Since impulsivity is common in children with ODD, it's absolutely essential to take any and all precautions with regards to safety.

Violence is a common means for children with ODD to express their intense emotions. Though it's not very helpful and often lands them in trouble, it's a way for them to release overwhelming feelings. Between enduring intense discomfort and getting relief, relief wins nearly every time—even when it's at someone else's expense. That's why helping ODD kids find alternatives to their aggressive impulses is so important. You can usually predict violence by learning to identify your child's triggers. Once you do, you may be able to help your child significantly reduce their violent outbursts. Let's examine how and where violence presents and what you can do to de-escalate.

At Home

A child who engages in kicking, hitting, biting, pushing, throwing things, or destroying property can make your home feel like a battleground. Though not all children with ODD use violence, most resort to it on some occasions. Your child's violent behavior is likely more impulsive and intense than that of their siblings. It can leave you and your other children feeling intimidated or fearful.

When there's violence in the home, it's common for family members to appease or tiptoe around the aggressor. Unfortunately, this gives the person with the least impulse control the most power. It's more effective to learn your child's triggers and behavioral cues so you can intervene early when you notice their mood beginning to shift.

If you can identify subtle signs—a shift in vocal tone, reddening of the face, fidgeting—that commonly precede outbursts, you can interrupt the escalation cycle with distractions like asking your child an off-topic question or bringing up a recent story you've heard. One of my clients noticed her son would start to shake his leg rapidly before eruptions, so she learned to jump in with a question about sports (his favorite subject) whenever she saw him shaking his leg. It worked at least half the time, which we all considered a major success. You might also remind your child of alternative behaviors such as taking a pause when you see them becoming frustrated. Trying to defuse the situation *before* they erupt will have a far better outcome.

Helping your child learn to manage their extreme behaviors may require you to take some calculated but serious steps such as involving law enforcement or even hospitalizing them until they're no longer a danger to others. This is more common in older children, who pose a greater threat of inflicting major harm. While doing so should always be a last resort, there are times when it's necessary to maintain safety.

At School

Violence at school is of great concern not just because of the safety risk to all involved but also because your child might be suspended or expelled. Age plays a key role in how schools handle violence; a five-year-old who strikes their peer is very different from a fifteen-year-old who does the same. No matter their age, if your child is demonstrating violence at school, they're likely being triggered by environmental factors, whether that's teachers, administrators, peers, or the curriculum itself. It's important to collaborate with school staff to figure out the context of the aggression.

While most parents dread calls home from school regarding their child's unruly behavior, consider those calls or meetings opportunities to gain more insight into your child's academic and social functioning. Though children with ODD are often aggressive, it's a mistake to assume they're bullies. They're more likely to *be* bullied because of their reactive behavior and impaired social skills. They make easy targets because bullies like to prey on kids they can get a rise out of. If your child is getting into fights, get more information on what's causing them. Though violence is never acceptable, if it's a reaction to being bullied, then the school should take steps to protect your child.

Graduated Interventions

This section will help you target extreme behaviors with lower-level, positive interventions before progressing to stricter measures. When possible, always try to use positive reinforcement, rewards, and extinction to positively shape behavior. However, with more extreme behaviors, especially those that threaten the safety and emotional well-being of others, logical consequences (consequences that don't happen automatically and require adult intervention) and punishments may be needed.

If your child's violence is dangerous, get your other children or yourself out of harm's way before using any of the interventions noted below. This is especially important with kids eleven and older. If they're a danger to themselves or others, please call 911 or take them to the nearest emergency room. This is not about punishment but about safety.

For all steps, keeping calm is essential. If your child is escalated, responding with anger or panic will only escalate them further. I know it's hard, but you can do it!

Graduated Intervention 1:
At the first sign of violence, calmly validate your child's feelings, state the rules regarding violence, and offer an alternative behavior. ("I know you're mad. We keep our hands to ourselves in this family. Maybe taking a break will help.") Don't try to reason with them; they can't access that part of their brain when they're triggered, and it'll likely only exacerbate the situation. Calmly repeat the rule twice, using the exact same language each time.

If they stop or pause their aggressive actions, positively reinforce them: "I can tell you're really trying to manage your feelings." Offer space or connection. For younger kids, "Do you need a hug or some alone time?" often works. For older kids: "I'm here if you need me, but I'm going to give you some space." Give your child time to cool off before talking about the outburst. If your child doesn't cool down, then proceed to graduated intervention 2.

Graduated Intervention 2:

If your child's behavior is uncontrollable, a logical consequence becomes necessary. Remind them of the boundary you've stated and alternative behaviors, and then calmly state the consequence for their behavior if it persists. For example, "Hitting your sister is not okay. You have the choice to walk away now or miss out on the movies this weekend." Whatever consequence you choose, you must follow through with it.

Calmly use the same phrase twice, waiting a moment between each repetition for them to hear you. If they stop, then proceed with positive reinforcement, validating their good choice and offering space for them to calm down. Again, do not attempt a lecture until they've completely de-escalated. If they continue acting out violently, proceed to graduated intervention 3.

Graduated Intervention 3:

If your initial attempts to get your child to stop using violence do not succeed, then you must put a barrier between them and their target(s) and decide if you need to contact the police.

Most kids will tire out and either retreat or break down emotionally. If this happens, let them de-escalate, checking on them as needed. After they've completely calmed down, debrief with them. Remind them of the boundary, their alternatives for next time, and finally the consequence. Let them know you love them and that your job is to keep everyone safe: "We settle things peacefully in this house. I know you were angry at your brother. Maybe next time you could pet the dog for a few minutes before you react. Since you chose to continue hitting him after we talked, you're not going to be able to play your video game tonight. I love you, and it's my responsibility to keep everyone safe."

These graduated interventions can help you give your child options before rushing to punishment. As with any intervention, please focus first on safety.

Verbal and Psychological Abuse

Verbal aggression and psychological abuse are common in children with ODD. Verbal aggression includes screaming, yelling, not letting the other person speak, and any other attempts to dominate and control a person verbally. Psychological abuse occurs when someone attacks or attempts to gain control over another by demeaning, threatening, manipulating, or gaslighting them. Verbal and psychological abuse can be precursors to physical violence, so it's important to take these behaviors seriously.

If a child exhibits verbally abusive behaviors, that doesn't mean they're a bad kid. Their cruel words are usually a sign of impulse and emotion-regulation problems. Remember that they're passing the "hot potato" as a means of managing their overwhelming internal experience. That said, it's not okay for them to be verbally or psychologically abusive. Let's review how these behaviors can present at home and school and then strategize ways to intervene.

At Home

You're sitting at home on a quiet Saturday afternoon when suddenly you hear commotion upstairs. As you approach, you hear your child with ODD screaming at their sibling, "You're such an idiot! I told you I wanted to play first. I hate you!" Does this sound familiar? Having an explosive child who lashes out verbally is stressful. Their behavior shatters the peace at home and tears down whoever's on the receiving end of their wrath. The old "sticks and stones" adage is wrong—words really can hurt you.

Seeking Professional Support

Helping your child learn to manage their ODD symptoms is not easy! You can definitely create positive change in your child's life, but it may also be necessary to seek professional help for your child and/or yourself, particularly in the following situations:

- *Your child is a danger to themselves or others. This includes threats of suicide.*
- *Your child is engaging in self-harm behaviors like cutting, hitting, banging, or scratching themselves.*
- *You notice your older child talking to themselves or responding to something you cannot see or hear.*
- *Your child's behavior continues to escalate or plateaus, despite your best efforts.*
- *Your child has learning difficulties at school.*
- *Due to your child's behavior, they face severe consequences such as being expelled or arrested.*
- *You suspect that something besides ODD is influencing their behavior, such as depression, anxiety, a learning disability, or substance/alcohol abuse.*

It's always wise to involve your child's pediatrician in their mental health treatment and to assess for any biological basis for their behaviors. Psychologists, marriage and family therapists, social workers, or other professionals trained in counseling can be great resources for treating ODD, depression, anxiety, and other mental health conditions that may be influencing your child. Psychologists can also perform psychological, cognitive, neuropsychological, and learning disorder assessments to determine if your child has identifiable problems in any of these areas. Your child's school may be able to provide resources for assessment of learning disabilities or other school-related challenges. Consulting with a child psychiatrist may be useful to determine if your child could benefit from medications.

When it comes to seeking professional support, don't forget about yourself. Helping your child learn to manage their ODD symptoms is a major task. If you're experiencing feelings of depression or becoming overwhelmed, speak with your physician and possibly a therapist. Support groups for parents can help normalize your experience; Facebook and other social media sites are a great starting place for such groups. If you or your child needs extra support, please don't put off finding it.

Or perhaps your ODD child is older and more adept at using words as weapons. They might say something like, "If you ground me, I'm going to kill myself." How do you know whether the threat is idle or not? In cases like this, it's common for adolescents with ODD to gain the upper hand because their parents are so fearful. This is an example of the psychological abuse you may be experiencing at the hands of your child. Though these behaviors are probably tied to a skills deficit in emotion regulation, they're still frightening and coercive.

At School

If you're like many parents of children with ODD, you've likely had your share of calls and emails from their teacher to discuss your child's verbal aggression. Though not all ODD kids act out at school, many do, since the skill set they lack doesn't discriminate between home and school. I had a client who was expelled from all three private kindergartens in her area for verbally threatening her peers. Your child's verbal aggression can land them in almost as much trouble as physically violent behaviors, especially in the school setting.

I worked with a client named Tyler who would complain about kids at school. He'd describe how he wanted to "jump them" or "kick their asses" until I reminded him of my status as a mandated reporter: I'm legally required to report to authorities if a client has made a credible threat of violence, as well as to warn the potential victim(s) themselves. Since Tyler hadn't used any names, I didn't have enough information to report, but it started a great conversation about the weight of our words. He was obviously concerned I was going to call the police and immediately backtracked, assuring me he'd never "kicked anyone's ass" and was "just mad." We spent the remainder of the session working on more appropriate ways to express his feelings that wouldn't result in police questioning.

No parent wants a call home about their child's abusive behavior, and it can be stressful and embarrassing to be told of their latest outburst. Still, the school can become an ally in reducing your child's defiance. I highly encourage you to seek resources from the school in the form of counseling, testing, and any accommodations that can be made to help your child succeed. It takes a village to treat ODD.

Graduated Interventions

These graduated interventions are aimed at using the ABCs to help you manage your child's verbally aggressive behaviors.

Graduated Intervention 1:

When your child becomes verbally abusive, calmly validate their feelings, state the boundary for communication, and offer an alternative behavior: "You're clearly angry, and we still speak to each other respectfully. Maybe you can go get a glass of water." Calmly repeat the boundary and the alternative, using the exact same language, twice more.

If your child makes a better choice, ceases their verbal assault, or decreases their aggression, positively reinforce them: "I can see you're really working hard to make better choices." Offer them space or connection, and let them cool off before talking about the outburst. If their behavior doesn't de-escalate, proceed to graduated intervention 2.

Graduated Intervention 2:
Calmly, in a neutral tone, remind your child of the boundary and alternatives, then add the consequence if their behavior persists: "We speak to each other respectfully here. If you don't want to go get a drink or take space, then you won't be able to watch YouTube after dinner." Remember to follow through with the consequence if they don't change their behavior.

Calmly and slowly repeat the phrase twice. If they stop, proceed with positive reinforcement and offer space or connection. If they persist, proceed to graduated intervention 3.

Graduated Intervention 3:
Try to remove any reinforcement of the problematic behavior. If your kid is yelling at a sibling, have the sibling go to their room or go play outside. If you're the target of their aggression, completely ignore the behavior until it ceases. Remember, for these children even negative attention is rewarding and thus reinforces the behavior. Once they've stopped their assault, praise their "good choice" and wait for them to fully de-escalate. After that period, remind them of the boundary and the consequence you laid out: "We do not call each other names, and you will not be able to go with me to the mall this afternoon." When the time is right, debrief with your child on the experience and alternatives they could try next time they get triggered.

Acting Out in Public

"Tantrum on aisle five." "Meltdown in the shoe department." Ever feel like this might as well be playing over the PA system when your child has a public outburst? For many parents, these are the most difficult scenarios to endure, probably because of the feelings of shame and self-consciousness they experience when their child "loses it" in front of others. Not only are they frustrated and worried, they're also cringing inwardly at the thought of everyone looking on and judging.

Last year at the county fair, my son had an epic tantrum. At one point he even kicked a churro out of my hand, much to the horror of the moms nearby. I could feel my face become hot with embarrassment while thoughts of my parenting failures raced through my head. When it was over and I could reflect on the situation more clearly, I realized that my son's behavior was due to his inability to manage feeling overwhelmed by the large crowd and anxious about the rides. Though his aggression seemed like defiance, it was far from it—his stress level had simply overridden his coping capacity. Whatever the reason for your child's public outbursts, helping them to manage more adaptively will greatly benefit them.

When to Use Extinction

Figuring out when to intervene and when to simply ignore your child's problematic behavior can be tricky—doubly so in public. It's easier to ignore their outbursts when you're confined to the privacy of your home than when you're in a store or restaurant. I've heard some horror stories about very public fits of anger carried out by little (and not so little) people.

How do you know when to use extinction (ignoring the problematic actions) and when to correct or punish? First, consider the purpose or function of the behavior. If your child seems to want to avoid or control the situation, then extinction is useful. For example, if you know they hate grocery shopping and they're having a tantrum because they want to leave, you'd be better off going the extinction route, because you don't want to reinforce their acting out. However, if you're in the same situation and know your child's tantrum is because they're hungry, giving them a snack will be more useful than ignoring the behavior. There's a big difference between defiance and a physiological need for food.

If your child's disruptive behavior seems to be related to expressing their overwhelming feelings, then you can ignore the behavior and offer support when they stop yelling. This combines extinction with shaping and offers a more adaptive alternative behavior while not reinforcing the problematic one. For example, if your child is melting down at the grocery store because he's frustrated, you could say aloud, "I will be able to help Johnny when he talks in a quieter voice." You're offering assistance while not giving attention to the tantrum.

Using extinction in public may require you to dig deep into your patience reserves. Breathe deeply and repeat to yourself that it doesn't matter how many people are staring because what you're working on is far more important than your feelings of embarrassment. Repeat as needed.

The goal of extinction is to teach your child that negative or extreme behaviors will no longer get them the results they're looking for, so they need to choose a more adaptive behavior instead. This can be a painful process, but in conjunction with consistent positive reinforcement of desired actions, it can lead to lasting behavior change. Hang in there, and remember what you're working toward!

When to Use Punishment

There are times when punishment is a necessary intervention to reduce your child's more extreme behaviors. Though other means of changing behavior, namely positive reinforcement and extinction, are more effective and will be your go-to strategies, sometimes your child will need to experience a negative consequence. If they're acting out aggressively, damaging property, or harming others emotionally or physically, they may initially need to lose out on privileges or have things taken away to learn how their extreme actions can negatively impact them. I urge you to reserve this for the most extreme behaviors.

Punishments such as time-outs, loss of privileges, or grounding can work, but they need to be brief, mild, and administered *immediately* after the unwanted behavior. If you're going to take away their screen time, do it for the rest of the day, not a week. When it comes to younger kids, keep time-outs to five minutes or less, and during that time remove all reinforcement (even negative attention). Grounding your teen for a month won't reinforce their positive behaviors; grounding them over the weekend may prove more effective. Since holding to long-term punishments is hard for most parents, this also increases your chances of sustaining consistency.

When issuing punishments, remain calm and consistent. Don't issue punishments when angry. The goal is to help kids make better behavioral choices, not to scare or shame them. (Shame has no place in this program because it's always destructive.)

Finally, one of the least effective ways to positively shape behavior is to issue threats of punishment without following through. Once your child knows you'll cave, they'll do whatever it takes to get you to relent. The moment you do, your child becomes the one in charge.

I always advise against corporal punishment because I believe physical punishment is ineffective at teaching children new skills. Inflicting fear and pain in children may temporarily increase compliance, but it doesn't help them learn what to do instead or increase their motivation to do the right thing. Physical punishment also causes children to associate hitting or spanking with the punisher— typically the parent. This creates a state of tension, as the person who's supposed to instill feelings of safety also inflicts pain. Over time, this tension can erode the healthy bond between parent and child. If you personally disagree with this stance, I encourage you to experiment with other forms of consequences before spanking your child.

Remember to Take Care of You

You've been working this program for a while now, and it's time to check in to see how you're doing. Remember the depression and anxiety questionnaires you completed in chapter 2? I asked you to note your scores in your notebook so you could compare them to your future scores.

Take 10 minutes to complete the questionnaires again and write down your new scores and today's date. How do they compare? If you notice you're checking off more items on either scale, then it's time to assess if you need some extra support. If your scores have gone down, what do you attribute this to? Scores that go down are usually an indication that things are improving and/or you're gaining more tools for taking of yourself. Either way, it's a sign of progress!

If you find you're getting bored with your self-care routine, here are a few ways to mix it up:

- *Get creative! Do a craft, paint a picture, write a poem. It doesn't matter what the task is as long as it challenges you to express your creativity.*
- *Read something just for fun like a gossipy tabloid, feel-good stories of animal rescues, or a religious text. Relish taking in information that is purely for your enjoyment or to nourish your soul.*
- *Give back to others by donating your time, services, clothing, or household goods. Helping others, even sporadically, makes us feel better about ourselves and others.*

If your self-care routine has fallen off, no problem— today's a good day to get back on track. You don't need to spend a lot of time on self-care; you just need to be intentional about making yourself and your well-being a priority.

Graduated Interventions

Now that you have some new tools for managing your child's behaviors around violence and verbal abuse, let's focus on things to try when they act out in public.

Graduated Intervention 1:
When your child is acting out in public, first consider if extinction is appropriate. If they're not hurting anyone or damaging property, try ignoring their behavior. With younger children, you can say aloud, "Once Diana stops running around, I'll be able to hear her again." For older children and teens: "I'm not able to talk to you when you're being disrespectful to me in public." The trick with these phrases is not to say anything else and to repeat them only a couple times. Ignore all other behaviors, no matter how embarrassed you feel.

If the behavior persists for more than 10 minutes or escalates to a point at which extinction is no longer viable, proceed to graduated intervention 2.

Graduated Intervention 2:
If extinction doesn't work, calmly remind your child of the expectations for their behavior in public, offer alternatives, and then state the consequence if they don't make a better choice. "I expect you to stay seated at restaurants. You can either sit down in your chair or we'll have to take our food to go." Remember, use only consequences you can follow through on.

Calmly and slowly repeat the phrase twice. If your child stops, use positive reinforcement. If they persist in acting out, proceed to graduated intervention 3.

Graduated Intervention 3:
Remind your child of the expectation and the consequence, then swiftly institute the consequence. "We stay in our seats in restaurants. Because you did not stay seated, we now have to take our food to go." This is the part that can be a bummer for parents. You may have to leave restaurants, stores, or events. Still, these are powerful

opportunities to help shape kids' behavior for the better. It also lets them see there are immediate consequences for their actions.

Action Plan: Two-Week Intervention for Extreme Behavior

You now have three sets of graduated interventions aimed at targeting your child's most extreme behaviors. For the next two weeks, choose one set to implement based on the most troublesome or frequent behaviors.

Once you've chosen, talk with your child about the new plan. Let them know you want them to be able to manage things better and will be offering them tools when you notice they're beginning to go off track. Talk to them about boundaries and how they struggle with maintaining them sometimes. Discuss punishment and how you hope to avoid using it whenever possible, but there may be times when it's needed to help them grow.

Tailor the graduated intervention to your child and your family rules. The moment you notice your child engaging in the targeted behavior, immediately start with the first intervention. If you keep it written on an index card, then you won't have to rely on your memory when you're already stressed out. Proceed through each intervention as needed until the behavior ceases. After your child has de-escalated, perhaps even the next day, debrief with them and strategize how things can go differently next time.

Continue to focus on the graduated interventions for the targeted behaviors in two-week increments, extending the process as needed. Once you've noticed a marked reduction in one set of behaviors, start on the next for two weeks, until they, too, become manageable. Be patient with yourself. You're targeting your child's most extreme behaviors, so it won't be easy, but your time and consistency will pay off!

Takeaways

- Managing your child's extreme behaviors takes a toll on you and your whole family.
- Maintaining a cool, calm demeanor in these explosive situations is essential.
- Consistency, consistency, consistency! That's the key to managing violence, verbal aggression/abuse, and acting out publicly.
- If positive reinforcements don't work, then logical consequences and punishment may be needed.
- Choosing between punishment and extinction requires you to choose your battles in order to win the war.
- Using graduated interventions can help you when confronted with these severe symptoms.
- Don't forget to take care of yourself!

CHAPTER NINE

Your Path Forward

Long-Term Outlook

You'll always be your child's parent. Even when they're fully grown, you'll never stop guiding and supporting them. Age eighteen is not an expiration date on your opportunities to positively impact your child. Their growth is an ongoing, fluid process—and so is the treatment plan you've created. It will continue to change and evolve as you and your child both gain more skills and insight. What's hard today could become easier in a month. The goals you've set may seem like a far-fetched dream, but they could be reality in the not-so-distant future.

I know this is a lot of information. The methods in this book may seem challenging and time-consuming. It's a demanding program—but so is parenting a child with unmanaged ODD symptoms. This model takes a lot of consistency, and I get that it's hard to stay the course when you're under intense stress. You can do this, but you definitely need to give yourself grace and time.

In the beginning, it's normal if the tools don't seem like a good fit. You'll be clunky at instituting them initially, but as they become part of your daily lives, you and your child will begin using them more intuitively. They'll feel less contrived and more natural. You probably fell a lot when you were first learning to ride a bike, but now it feels like the most natural thing in the world. That's not because it was easy to learn but because you kept practicing.

I once worked with a family with a very defiant six-year-old named Logan. Each week, we'd work on skill building, consistency, and positive reinforcement, but it took a while for the parents to "buy in" to the concept of reducing punishments. In fact, they initially refused, believing that Logan was learning to "get away with" things. But as their ability to catch him doing well increased, their need to punish him sharply decreased. It was a natural evolution. When I pointed this out to them, they were surprised to realize they hadn't issued a punishment in over two weeks. This was both a family record and the fruit of their willingness to try something different. Six months later,

Logan continued to make progress, and the behavioral goals shifted. Though he was no longer overtly defiant, he was still rather inflexible. But since the defiance was now manageable, it became much easier to treat the rigidity. Logan, like the rest of us, was a work in progress. If you can approach this program as a fluid process, you'll find you can always adapt to your child's changing needs.

Targeting Your Biggest Challenges

As you know, a parent's work is never done. The behavior plans you created in previous chapters will one day be obsolete, with new ones taking their place. The action plans and treatment goals will need to be revised as your child progresses. Once your child has met a goal, or the weekly homework assignment is successfully completed, your job is to start over or refine the previous goal to sustain momentum. Find ways to collaborate with your child, allowing them more influence in selecting joint goals.

If you find your child is regressing from their gains or even taking one step forward and two steps back, that's a normal part of the learning process. It doesn't mean they're not changing; it simply highlights the need to remain consistent in implementing the program. I worked with a family for over a year in weekly sessions, and when their child got to the point where they no longer met the criteria for ODD, she asked, "What's next?" I loved her zest for change! There is no "completion date" for this work. With persistence and hard work, there may come a time when your child has their symptoms well managed, and you can set new goals aimed at helping them thrive instead of merely surviving. Stay the course.

Create a Template for Future Action Plans

As you've probably noticed, this program is active, structured, and goal-directed. Making lasting change is very intentional work. In that spirit, creating a template for future action plans is important because it will take the guesswork out of setting new goals and identifying the tools needed to achieve them.

The following steps are essential components of future action plans targeting unhelpful behaviors.

1. Target a behavior for change.
2. Identify what behavior you'd like to see instead.
3. Create SMART goals.
4. Identify boundaries (expectations, rules, or limits) for behavior.
5. Identify alternative behaviors to use instead of the target behavior.
6. Select consequences—praise, rewards, validation, extinction.

To clarify the process, I'll use the example of thirteen-year-old Ethan, who hates wasting his time on showering when he'd rather be playing video games. His parents have noticed his body odor and are concerned about his hygiene. Ethan doesn't care, but he also doesn't want to lose any video game time.

1. Target a behavior for change: Ethan doesn't shower daily and becomes defiant when prompted by his parents.
2. Identify what behavior you'd like to see instead: His parents want him to shower daily.
3. Create SMART goals: "Ethan will begin showering daily, with no more than one parental prompt within one week."
4. Identify boundaries for behavior: "In our house, we're responsible for maintaining our personal hygiene by showering and using deodorant daily."

5. Identify alternative behaviors to use instead of the target behavior: Ethan will set a time to shower daily. He will stop playing his video game 10 minutes before his scheduled shower. He will consider his choices before refusing to shower. He will do 10 push-ups to reduce frustration if his frustration is over a level three because he has to shower.

6. Select consequences: Ethan will get 15 extra minutes of video game time on Friday and Saturday nights for successfully showering every day of the previous week. His parents will praise his efforts and willingness to follow the rules. His complaints about showering will be ignored by his parents rather than argued about (extinction).

After creating an action plan from the template, remember to do the following:

- Schedule regular check-ins to make sure you're remaining on target, and write down progress in your notebook.
- Brainstorm about what is and isn't working, and strategize about how to remove obstacles.
- When the goal is completed, check in with your child to determine if the goal can be revised for further growth or if you should set a new goal.

This formula will be your guide for future goal setting. The following exercise is your opportunity to put this template to work.

EXERCISE: Create an Action Plan with Your Child

I'm assuming that you and your child have made some positive changes by this point in the program. Don't forget to acknowledge that effort and success. In order to capitalize on your joint effort, invite your child to collaborate on an action plan for the next month.

In your notebook, work together to come up with the following:

1. Target a behavior for change.
2. Identify what behavior you'd like to see instead.
3. Create SMART goals.
4. Identify boundaries (expectations, rules, or limits) for behavior.
5. Identify alternative behaviors to use instead of the target behavior.
6. Select consequences—praise, rewards, validation, extinction.

Once you've written down these steps, pull out your calendar and schedule weekly check-ins with your child to gauge their progress. During these weekly meetings, discuss growth and areas where you need to focus more attention next week. Write down progress in your notebook, and at the end of the month, meet to determine if the goal has been successfully completed or if you need to extend the process. Once the goal has been attained (even if before the one-month mark), collaborate on a new goal for the following month. Remember, this is a fluid process, and there will always be something to work on. Keep up the good work!

Finding What Works for You

There is no magic bullet for ODD. Strategies that work for one child may fail miserably for another. That's why I've tried to provide a variety of interventions for you to test out. This model is based on a conceptual framework with very strong research support, but the individual skills that are most effective for you and your child will vary. Don't be discouraged by the process of elimination necessary to figure out what does or doesn't work in relation to coping skills. If it were easy, you would've done it a long time ago and would not have needed this book.

The best coping strategies are ones that are actually used. My favorite coping skill to help my clients with emotion regulation and distress tolerance is deep breathing, because there's lots of research to support its efficacy in resetting the nervous-system response. Still, there are occasionally some clients this technique doesn't work for. One could argue that maybe the client is doing it wrong or isn't really trying, but what's important is that they're not using it, so for them it's not an effective coping skill, and our time will be much more productive if I offer them different skills. You don't need a lot of them, though—just a handful that work and that you don't mind using. If certain tools aren't working for you or your child, drop them and try something else. There are far too many good and practical skills that *can* work to get hung up on ones that don't.

I worked with a young girl, Halleh, who was extremely defiant at home and school. Fortunately, she was an angel in my office. We always had a great time working on coping skills in sessions, but it soon became apparent that she wouldn't use them outside of session. When I asked why, she said she didn't like when her parents or teacher "bossed her around" by telling her to use her skills. Though her caregivers were trying to help her by giving her reminders, she, in all her prickliness, interpreted the help as "bossiness." This created a power struggle that she was determined to win. Though I often tell parents to encourage the use of coping skills, for this little girl (and many others like her) that simply didn't work.

Plan B was collaborating with Halleh and her parents on ways she could more readily use the tools she'd learned. I suggested that they give her the opportunity to voluntarily use a skill before they intervened. This alone was a skill. If after two minutes she didn't do so, then her parents could tap their temple and say, "Shake, shake, shake," signaling to her to use a coping strategy. (Halleh was a big

Taylor Swift fan, so I knew choosing lyrics from one of her songs would be a less frustrating prompt.) Within a few weeks, she was using her skills more often and of her own accord. Her parents reported that she needed the prompt only a handful of times, and there were fewer power struggles overall because they had been flexible in trying different skills until they found one that was effective for Halleh. Had we continued with the original plan, we'd probably still be stuck.

Tools don't have to be overly complicated or prescribed by a professional to be helpful. If you notice that your child seems calmer when they're drawing, that can become a useful tool to increase their self-soothing abilities. I even have one client who likes to make slime as a way to manage his anxiety. Figure out things your child is already doing to feel better, and turn those into strategies for handling their intense feelings.

If you're stumped for skills, there are many options online. Though I have a whole library of treatment manuals and subscribe to several academic journals, I've adopted many of my favorite skills from the Internet. If you Google a phrase like "coping skills for children," "emotion regulation skills for kids," or "anger management strategies for adolescents," you'll find a wealth of choices. Remember, there's no one-size-fits-all tool or strategy, so don't feel bad if some fall flat. The more flexible you can be in honing your child's treatment plan, the more success you'll have in reaching your goals.

Staying on Track

Remember, consistency is key in helping your child manage their ODD symptoms. Your best bet for making lasting changes is to stay on track with taking care of yourself, sticking to the treatment plan, and using the ABCs and other tools you've learned. This might mean enlisting the support of a partner or friend to help you remain accountable when you feel like giving up. It might mean making changes to the family schedule or establishing new routines. You may find it useful to set reminders for certain tasks in your phone (I find the app Productive handy for this).

If you get off track, don't freak out. You can always start again or pick up where you left off. Though it can be more challenging because defiance flourishes when things aren't consistent, change is still possible. If you've fallen off the wagon, before you jump back on, take some time to consider what obstacles made staying on track difficult. Create a plan to manage those roadblocks differently next time. For example, if your child's activity schedule made it hard to create a routine, then maybe they can take a break from some activities while you do the very important work of helping them manage their ODD more adaptively. Or if you're having trouble managing your reactivity because you're under intense stress, perhaps you can prioritize your well-being by seeing a therapist or taking a stress-management class. Whatever the obstacles that derailed your work, if you can identify them and mitigate their impact with some contingency planning, then you should be able to get back on the right track.

EXERCISE: Goal Setting

At this point in the program, your child has probably learned a lot about setting goals and working toward them. Now's the time to further foster their development in this area. Using the following format, invite your child to collaborate on creating a relationship goal that you can work on together.

1. Target a behavior for change (for example, you don't spend enough time together).
2. Identify what behavior you'd like to see instead (for example, you want more quality time together each week).
3. Create SMART goals. ("We will spend at least 10 minutes snuggling, talking, or playing together before bed at least five times per week within one month.")

4. Schedule weekly check-ins to see if you're on target and identify obstacles. Note the progress in your notebook.
5. At the end of the time line, reconvene and determine if you want to continue with the goal, revise it, or create a new goal.

This exercise is intended to be a fun way to work toward your parent-child relationship goals together while also helping your child build their goal-planning skills with your guidance and support. I hope you both enjoy it!

Finding Support

The purpose of this book is to help you provide tools to your child so they can better manage their ODD symptoms. If at this point in the reading you've found that your child is not responding or that you need some extra support, don't be discouraged. ODD is a challenging and complicated mental health condition that often co-occurs with other disorders. If that's the case for your child, then you'll likely need to seek outside support. That doesn't mean you failed; it means you've recognized that more resources are needed to create the necessary structure and consistency. Whatever the case, I urge you not to delay in accessing additional support. With ODD interventions, time is of the essence. In the next two sections, I'll review ways you can get started seeking out help.

Therapists and Other Specialists

It's not uncommon for children with ODD to need more intensive, focused care. If you feel your child is not making the gains you were hoping for, or their symptoms are increasing, meet with your child's pediatrician to rule out a physiological cause for their behavior, and assess whether a medication consultation with a child psychiatrist

Remember to Take Care of You

You've come a long way! When you first started this journey, self-care may have seemed like an impractical indulgence. It may still feel like a foreign concept at times, but hopefully you're incorporating it into your daily life. Your self-care routine may always be a work in progress, and that's okay. The goal is to persist in finding ways to care for your emotional, spiritual, and physical needs. Remember, when you put on your oxygen mask first, you'll be better able to care for your child's needs.

Think for a moment about your self-care regimen. Are you knocking it out of the park, or do you need to get back on track? In your notebook, write down two ways you've successfully incorporated taking care of you into your life. After that, jot down two obstacles that make self-care activities challenging. Finally, brainstorm (in your notebook) ways to increase your consistency with practicing self-care. For example, could you set reminders on your phone or schedule a walk with a friend every week?

If you're finding it hard to get time alone, here are some ways you can incorporate your children or spouse into some of your activities:

- *Start a gratitude post on social media, and ask friends and family to post one thing they're grateful for. You go first!*
- *Watch your favorite comedy with someone else—whatever makes you laugh out loud.*
- *Go outside at dusk with your family and encourage each person to make a wish on the first star in the sky.*

CONTINUED

- *Create a family vision board by cutting out images from magazines of things you'd like to do, places you'd like to go, or inspirational quotes. Get your partner or kids in on it, and display it somewhere you can all see it.*
- *Go out to a restaurant you haven't tried before with your significant other or a friend. Enjoy the grown-up conversation and savor the new fare.*
- *Write a thank-you card to someone in your household. For example, if your child put the wet clothes from the washer into the dryer, write a quick note of thanks expressing why it was meaningful to you.*
- *Gather the family or just your partner to watch the sunrise or sunset.*
- *Get out the crayons and color with your kids. Feel free to color outside the lines.*

Self-care is essential not only to this program but also to your overall wellness. Continue to make yourself a priority! You're worth it.

is warranted. Though many parents are hesitant to medicate their children, it helps to understand your options.

I also encourage you to seek the services of a child and adolescent therapist, psychologist, marriage and family therapist, or licensed clinical social worker who is specially trained in treating children with behavioral disorders and using cognitive behavioral therapy (CBT). If you've already come this far and your child remains stuck, you may need a specialist. While there are many models for treating children and adolescents, CBT will likely yield the best results and has decades of outstanding research support.

You can ask for referrals from your child's pediatrician, school, or friends/family members who have had similar challenges. You can also search online directories and sites like Psychologytoday.com for CBT therapists in your area.

A therapist will assess your child, make a diagnosis, create a treatment plan, and consult with their school and other providers throughout treatment. They will provide therapy, likely on a weekly basis. You will be a big part of treatment, and they'll probably even have parent-only sessions from time to time. You'll also want to work with your child on the skills they learn in session throughout the week. I'm always straightforward with parents about my role as a therapist. Therapists cannot "fix" your child, but they can be helpful guides to providing both you and your child with the skills and tools needed to change.

In some cases, therapists may recommend more intensive services, such as referring your child to a group program. This indicates the therapist believes your child's symptoms will be better treated in a different setting. Therapists have a legal and ethical obligation to refer clients out when a client's condition falls outside of their scope of competence or the client is not making the expected improvements. A good therapist won't allow your child to stay stuck in their care.

Support Groups: Online and In Person

Parenting a child with ODD is no simple task! It can be intensely stressful and isolating. Many parents have told me they feel like other parents can't relate—and they're right. Unless you have a child with ODD, you don't know the pain of seeing them struggle through life while also feeling overwhelmed by them. If you need some extra support as well, don't delay in reaching out.

I love parent support groups because they can normalize the challenges of parenting while also offering a respite from the chaos.

Whether you choose an online or in-person group really depends on availability in your area as well as your schedule. If you can't find a parent group specifically focused on ODD, you might try one for ADHD, since the two share a lot of the same behavioral problems. You can also try to start a group yourself by talking to local therapists who specialize in ODD. They may be willing to facilitate a group as a resource for parents of their clients. Any measure you take to access resources for you or your child will help out your cause. Taking these steps requires bravery and insight, and I'm confident that you have both.

Onward and Upward!

You've come to the end of this book, but it is by no means the end of your family's journey. You probably purchased the book because you wanted to understand your child and help them gain the skills to thrive in this world. I sincerely hope that it has been helpful in both areas. If you hold on to nothing else from this book, let it be this: Always stay hopeful. Both you and your child are intensely resilient, and your family now has the tools it needs to change for the better.

Resources

AACAP.org's Oppositional Defiant Disorder Resource Center
The ODD Resource Center on the American Academy of Child & Adolescent Psychology website offers great information and resources for parents.

American Psychiatric Association (Psychiatry.org)
The American Psychiatric Association website provides information on ODD and other psychiatric conditions as well as resources for consumers.

American Psychological Association (APA.org)
The American Psychological Association website has a wealth of resources on mental health conditions, including ODD.

***The Explosive Child* by Ross W. Greene**
This is a great book that gives insight into the skills deficits your child may be experiencing as well as tools for collaborating with them to more effectively problem-solve. The companion website, **livesinthebalance.org**, offers resources for parents and teachers.

***The Kazdin Method for Parenting the Defiant Child* by Alan E. Kazdin**
This is a great book to help you further hone your skills in parenting your child with ODD.

National Alliance on Mental Illness (NAMI.org)
NAMI is a fantastic organization that advocates for those with mental health conditions and can be a great resource for information and support.

***Positive Discipline* by Jane Nelsen**
This is one of my favorite books on discipline and positive reinforcement. The companion website, **positivediscipline.com**, has tools and other resources for parents.

References

American Academy of Child & Adolescent Psychiatry. "Oppositional Defiant Disorder Resource Center." Accessed November 23, 2018. https://www.aacap.org/AACAP/Families_and_Youth/Resource _Centers/Oppositional_Defiant_Disorder_Resource_Center /Home.aspx.

American Psychiatric Association. *Diagnostic and Statistical Manual of Mental Disorders* (5th ed.). Arlington, VA: American Psychiatric Publishing, 2013.

Association for Contextual Behavior Science. "ACT." Accessed November 23, 2018. https://contextualscience.org/print/book /export/html/10.

Bach, Patricia A., Daniel J. Moran, and Steven C. Hayes. *ACT in Practice: Case Conceptualization in Acceptance & Commitment Therapy*. Oakland: New Harbinger Publications, 2008.

Bernstein, Jeffrey. *10 Days to a Less Defiant Child*. Boston: Da Capo Press, 2015.

Boyes, Alice. "Why Avoidance Coping is the Most Important Factor in Anxiety." Last modified March 5, 2013. https://www .psychologytoday.com/intl/blog/in-practice/201303/why-avoidance -coping-is-the-most-important-factor-in-anxiety.

Cannon, Megan A. "The Relationship among Attention Deficit/ Hyperactivity Disorder (ADHD) Subtypes, Oppositional Defiant Disorder (ODD), and Parenting Stress." PhD diss., Nova Southeastern University, 2013. ProQuest (3630823).

Chapman, Susan Gillis. *The Five Keys to Mindful Communication*. Boulder, CO: Shambhala, 2012.

Duncan, Larissa G., J. Douglas Coatsworth, and Mark T. Greenberg. "A Model of Mindful Parenting: Implications for Parent–Child

Relationships and Prevention Research." *Clinical Child and Family Psychology Review* 12, no. 3 (September 2009): 255–70. https://doi.org/10.1007/s10567-009-0046-3.

Fisher, Doug and Nancy Frey. *Unstoppable Learning: Seven Essential Elements to Unleash Student Potential.* Bloomington, IN: Solution Tree Press, 2015.

Gilbert, Elaine A.T. "Influence of the Parent-Child Relationship Quality on ADHD and ODD Symptom Severity." PsyD diss., Indiana State University, 2017. US: ProQuest (10602579).

Greene, Ross W. *The Explosive Child.* New York, NY: HarperCollins, 2005.

Hall, Bryan J. "The Process of Parenting Oppositional and Defiant Children." PhD diss., Capella University, 2015. ProQuest (3717992).

Hayes, Steven C., Kirk D. Strosahl, and Kelly G. Wilson. *Acceptance and Commitment Therapy: The Process and Practice of Mindful Change* (2nd ed). New York: The Guilford Press, 2012.

Judge, Lorna, Ailish Cleghorn, Kirsten McEwan, and Paul Gilbert. "An Exploration of Group-Based Compassion Focused Therapy for a Heterogeneous Range of Clients Presenting to a Community Mental Health Team." *International Journal of Cognitive Therapy* 5, no. 4 (December 2012): 420–29. https://doi.org/10.1521/ijct.2012.5.4.420.

Kashdan, Todd B., Rolf G. Jacob, William E. Pelham, Alan R. Lang, Betsy Hoza, Jonathan D. Blumenthal, and Elizabeth M. Gnagy. "Depression and Anxiety in Parents of Children with ADHD and Varying Levels of Oppositional Defiant Behaviors: Modeling Relationships with Family Functioning." *Journal of Clinical & Adolescent Psychology* 33, no. 1 (2004): 169–81. https://doi.org/10.1207/S15374424JCCP3301_16.

Kazdin, Alan E. *The Kazdin Method for Parenting the Defiant Child.* New York: Mariner Books, 2008.

Killingsworth, Matthew A. and Daniel T. Gilbert. "A Wandering Mind Is an Unhappy Mind." *Science* 330, no. 6006 (November 2010): 932. https://doi.org/10.1126/science.1192439.

Koons, Cedar R. *The Mindfulness Solution for Intense Emotions: Take Control of Borderline Personality Disorder with DBT*. Oakland: New Harbinger Publications, 2016.

LaVigna, Gary W. and Anne M. Donnellan. *Alternatives to Punishment: Solving Behavior Problems with Non-Aversive Strategies*. New York: Irvington Publishers, 1986.

Lin, Xiuyun, Yulin Zhang, Peilian Chi, Wan Ding, Melissa A. Heath, Xiaoyi Fang, and Shousen Xu. "The Mutual Effect of Marital Quality and Parenting Stress on Child and Parent Depressive Symptoms in Families of Children with Oppositional Defiant Disorder." *Frontiers in Psychology* 20, no. 8 (October 2017): 1810. https://doi.org/10.3389/fpsyg.2017.01810.

National Institute of Mental Health. "5 Things You Should Know About Stress." Accessed November 23, 2018. https://www.nimh.nih.gov/health/publications/stress/index.shtml.

National Scientific Council on the Developing Child. "Children's Emotional Development Is Built into the Architecture of their Brains: Working Paper No. 2." 2004. http://developingchild.harvard.edu/wp-content/uploads/2004/04/Childrens-Emotional-Development-Is-Built-into-the-Architecture-of-Their-Brains.pdf.

Nelsen, Jane. "Natural Consequences." Accessed November 23, 2018. https://www.positivediscipline.com/articles/natural-consequences.

Omilion-Hodges, Leah M. and Nathan M. Swords. "Communication That Heals: Mindful Communication Practices from Palliative Care Leaders." *Health Communication* 31, no. 3 (2016): 328–35. https://doi.org/10.1080/10410236.2014.953739.

Pederson, Casey A. and Paula J. Fite. "The Impact of Parenting on the Associations between Child Aggression Subtypes and Oppositional

Defiant Disorder Symptoms." *Child Psychiatry & Human Development* 45, no. 6 (December 2014): 728–35. https://doi.org/10.1007/s10578-014-0441-y.

Reed, Florence D. DiGennaro and Benjamin J. Lovett. "Views on the Efficacy and Ethics of Punishment: Results from a National Survey." *International Journal of Behavioral Consultation and Therapy* 4, no. 1 (2007): 61–67. https://doi.org/10.1037/h0100832.

Ross, Christine N., Holly M. Blanc, Cheryl B. McNeil, Sheila M. Eyberg, and Toni L. Hembree-Kigin. "Parenting Stress in Mothers of Young Children with Oppositional Defiant Disorder and Other Severe Behavior Problems." *Child Study Journal* 28, no. 2 (1998): 93–110.

Semel Institute for Neuroscience and Human Behavior. "How Do You Cope?" Accessed November 23, 2018. https://www.semel.ucla.edu/dual-diagnosis-program/news_and_resources/how_do_you_cope.

Siegel, Daniel J. *The Mindful Brain: Reflection and Attunement in the Cultivation of Well-Being.* New York: W. W. Norton & Company, 2007.

Sommers-Spijkerman, M. P. J., H. R. Trompetter, K. M. G. Schreurs, and E. T. Bohlmeijer. "Compassion-Focused Therapy as Guided Self-Help for Enhancing Public Mental Health: A Randomized Controlled Trial." *Journal of Consulting and Clinical Psychology* 86, no. 2 (February 2018): 101–15. https://doi.org/10.1037/ccp0000268.

Tempelsman, Cathy Rindner. *Child-Wise.* New York: HarperCollins, 1995.

Wallace, Dustin P., Beth Woodford, and Mark Connelly. "Promoting Psychological Flexibility in Parents of Adolescents with Chronic Pain: Pilot Study of an 8-week Group Intervention." *Clinical Practice in Pediatric Psychology* 4, no. 4 (December 2016): 405–16. https://doi.org/10.1037/cpp0000160.

Whyte, William Hollingsworth. "Is Anybody Listening?" *Fortune,* September 1950.

Index

About the Author

Gina Atencio-MacLean, PsyD, is a licensed clinical psychologist based in Orange County, California. She received her doctoral degree in clinical psychology from Azusa Pacific University and specializes in treating children and adolescents with behavioral problems using cognitive behavioral therapy (CBT). It is her goal to help children and their families gain the tools needed to thrive. She is intensely optimistic and approaches her clinical work with a strengths-based approach. Dr. Atencio-MacLean is also a wife and the mother of a wild and vivacious boy and two wonderful adult stepdaughters.

Printed in the USA
CPSIA information can be obtained
at www.ICGtesting.com
LVHW021451160524
780487LV00006B/15